Somebody Ought to be Crying

The Unauthorized Autobiographical Memoir

also by
J.B. HOGAN

Tin Hollow
Fallen: A Short Story Collection
Bar Harbor: A Short Story Collection
The Rubicon: A Poetry Collection
Losing Cotton
Living Behind Time

Angels in the Ozarks
Forgotten Fayetteville and Washington County

Somebody Ought to be Crying

The Unauthorized Autobiographical Memoir

J.B. HOGAN

OTTERFORD

BENTONVILLE, ARKANSAS

OTTERFORD

An Imprint of Roan & Weatherford Publishing Associates, LLC
Bentonville, Arkansas
www.roanweatherford.com

Copyright © 2024 by J.B. Hogan

Library of Congress Cataloging-in-Publication Data
Names: Hogan, J.B., author.
Title: Somebody Ought to be Crying
Description: First Edition | Bentonville: Otterford, 2024.
Identifiers: LCCN: 2024947797 | ISBN: 979-8-89299-001-1 (trade paperback) |
ISBN: 979-8-89299-002-8 (eBook)
Subjects: | BISAC: BIOGRAPHY & AUTOBIOGRAPHY/Memoirs |
BIOGRAPHY & AUTOBIOGRAPHY/General |
LC record available at: https://lccn.loc.gov/2024947797

Otterford trade paperback edition November, 2024

Cover & Interior Design by Casey W. Cowan
Editing by Don Money & Amy Cowan

To my long-suffering friends and family.

Joseph "Dad" Gilbert and J. B. Hogan, 1947, Mayfield, AR, Reunion.
Photo by Walter Allen

Out of the Void and Into the Light... Sort of

THERE WAS A bright light with no color. Then lights from some long, deep black place. After that, colors, colors with no names. Next was a room, dark, brothers and sister there, sick with fever or something. Later, walking a dirt country road, me and a brother, scared by a thing in the woods. He said maybe a deer.

Then clear. Two brothers and the sister on a stage in a Christmas play, feeling proud. In summer, biggest brother thinking he cut me with his pocketknife but there was no blood, no cut. There was crying and yelling, but there wasn't a red place. Living in a new place, by the big road with cars and trucks, scary, and a snake crawling fast through the grass by our house, not a big house like the one before.

Hot day walking in soft dirt on a road in the country where my cousins lived, it was hot and my bigger cousin was with me, walking across a bridge with wooden tracks for cars and on up the road to a little old store with old men in front spitting on the ground, whittling wood, cutting pieces of brown stuff to chew for spitting.

Inside was grandpa. He was tall, in the store by the glass candy jars and the soda pop in the big box with chunks of cold ice you could see through. Candy and soda pop for me and my cousin, from grandpa. He smiled and was gray and great big tall, way up over us like a giant, but not scary and good to us.

"Dad" Gilbert and Martha Hogan, Fayetteville, AR, ca. 1949.
J. B. Hogan Collection

Moving to Town

THE FIRST HOUSE in town was 1404 North Glendale. My momma taught me that. It had upstairs and downstairs and was above the railroad tracks. It was at the bottom of a hill down a dirt road with rocks all in it. A boy came down that hill on his bicycle one time and crashed, and he was tore up and bleeding all over. His red blood was on his arms and hands and face. He was hurt but he didn't cry.

I was hurt once, too. In the snow, I bent down to make a snowball and when I stood up there was a board with a nail stuck to my rear end. The nail was in my rear end. That hurt. It didn't seem funny and I cried. The doctor cleaned my rear and gave me a shot that made me feel funny for a while.

There was a dream. I was running along a little path with something after me. I ran and ran and ran but couldn't get away. It kept after me no matter what I did or how fast I ran. When I got to a bridge, I turned around and saw that the thing that was after me was the devil. I ran to the edge of the bridge. The devil was there, waiting to jump me. Below the bridge was water, cool and good. I kept looking at the water and the devil went away. I saw myself peeing over the rail of the bridge. When I woke up, my pants were all wet, and I was cold.

The living room was warm and dry. Saturday nights we went in there and listened to the radio. I lay in front of the radio and heard the Grand Old Opry. There was somebody called Little Jimmy Dickens and another man named Roy who sang about a big bird with speckles on it. I was warm and dry and felt safe from bad things, like the devil.

One day in spring, a train came by with all kinds of soldier trucks and jeeps and things on it. The tracks were right there behind our house. When me and my brother saw soldiers on some of the train cars we squealed and hollered and waved. The soldiers waved back. Our mother said they might be going to Korea. Korea was communists, and if I ate my peas like they were communist soldiers, I would grow up to be a big, strong man and we would win the war.

On a Saturday, my brothers and me were going to go to the movies uptown. It was a Ma and Pa Kettle movie. That would be funny. We walked up the railroad tracks to the first paved road, but we saw rain coming across the hills off away from town and my brothers said, "Hurry, we have to get back home before the rain hits." You could see it coming across the hills like in a wave or a sheet. It was something.

"Hurry, run!" They yelled, but I couldn't move. "What's the matter with you?"

"I don't know how to run." I cried.

They were laughing, and they grabbed me by the arms and drug me down the tracks to our house. The rain came right on top of us. It was coming down fast and hard. We were wet all through our clothes to our bodies by the time we got home. I didn't mean to get us wet, but I couldn't help it, I completely forgot how to run.

Truman, MacArthur, and a Flight of Geese

THE SECOND HOUSE in town was above City Park. I think its address was 512 Edgewood, but I don't know for sure. It was smaller than the big house back down by the tracks, but it was warm and cozy. My grandfather, my mother's daddy, sat in an easy chair in the living room. He was old and didn't feel good very much. His name was Joseph Gilbert. We called him Dad. Dad Gilbert. He was tall and good. He ate the food I didn't want.

I drank my chocolate milk, though. It came with the milkman in the morning and was in a cold bottle with water on the outside of the bottle, and it had a paper cap that I peeled off and drank the sweet, brown milk. I ate skillet toast and the yellow part of eggs, and Dad Gilbert ate the rest. My mother said, "You'll spoil him, Dad." But grandpa didn't say anything about it. He let me sit by him in his big chair and patted me on the head.

I was like Dad in another way, too. I felt bad a lot. My head was real hot, and my nose was stopped up so that I couldn't barely breathe. I laid in bed and my legs hurt. Sometimes they hurt so bad I would stretch them as far as I could and for as long as I could and then let go. For a minute they wouldn't hurt that way.

When I felt better, my mother would read to me. She read me books about a little train that could and about a puppy and things like that. Her teeth were small and they went up and down when she read. I liked for her to read. Sometimes she read the newspaper to me. She let me read the books and the newspaper, too, sometimes, and I learned to say the words on the pages. It was fun. She told me I was a smart boy.

One time one of my uncles came to see us. He had been gone away somewhere for a long time. It was the only time I had ever seen him. While he was there, the radio was all loud about Mr. Truman and General MacArthur. Mr. Truman made General MacArthur go away my uncle said. I don't think my uncle liked Mr. Truman for that.

One time we were outside and there was this loud honking noise, and we looked up and the whole sky was full of these big, gray geese. They were flying in these big Vs, like they were in formation my brothers said. I couldn't believe there was so many of them. They were everywhere in the sky. I'd never seen that kind of thing before.

Another day, it was sunny, but we were in the house anyway, and my big brother had a bee or a bug or something in a Mason jar, and he was trying to punch a hole in the lid to let the bug or something breathe. He was taking this ice pick and jabbing it down into the jar lid, making little holes in it. But he must've goofed up or something because he brought that ice pick right down onto his own hand and stuck it right into that skin that's like a web between your thumb and first finger.

The ice pick went right through that skin and stuck into the jar lid. At first, my brother kind of yelled "ow" or something like that, but, boy, then he cut loose a whole batch of words I never even heard before. I knew they were words he shouldn't have said because my grandpa called from the other room for my brother to stop using that kind of language in front of the boy, which I figured was me.

I don't remember all the bad words exactly, but I think he said something about a "son of a b..." something, and there was a "hell" in there of some kind, too, and I think he used "damn" and the god word together which Dad Gilbert told him was real bad and he should not say that. My brother kept up that bunch of new words anyway until he got the ice pick out of that web thing between his thumb and fingers and put some alcohol and a little bandage on the hole that he ice picked into his own hand.

He didn't get into much trouble when our mother got home but she told me not to use those words that my brother had. I wasn't sure why I couldn't say them but I decided it would be better if I didn't say them in front of my mom or my granddad. I saved them up for using later, though, and when I was playing by myself out in the yard or alone in the bathroom or some other place where nobody else was, I would say them real quiet to myself.

I figured there might be a time later when I could use words like that. They might come in handy, especially if you did something to yourself like sticking an ice pick in the web thing between your thumb and first finger. Especially then, you'd want words like that. Nothing else would do.

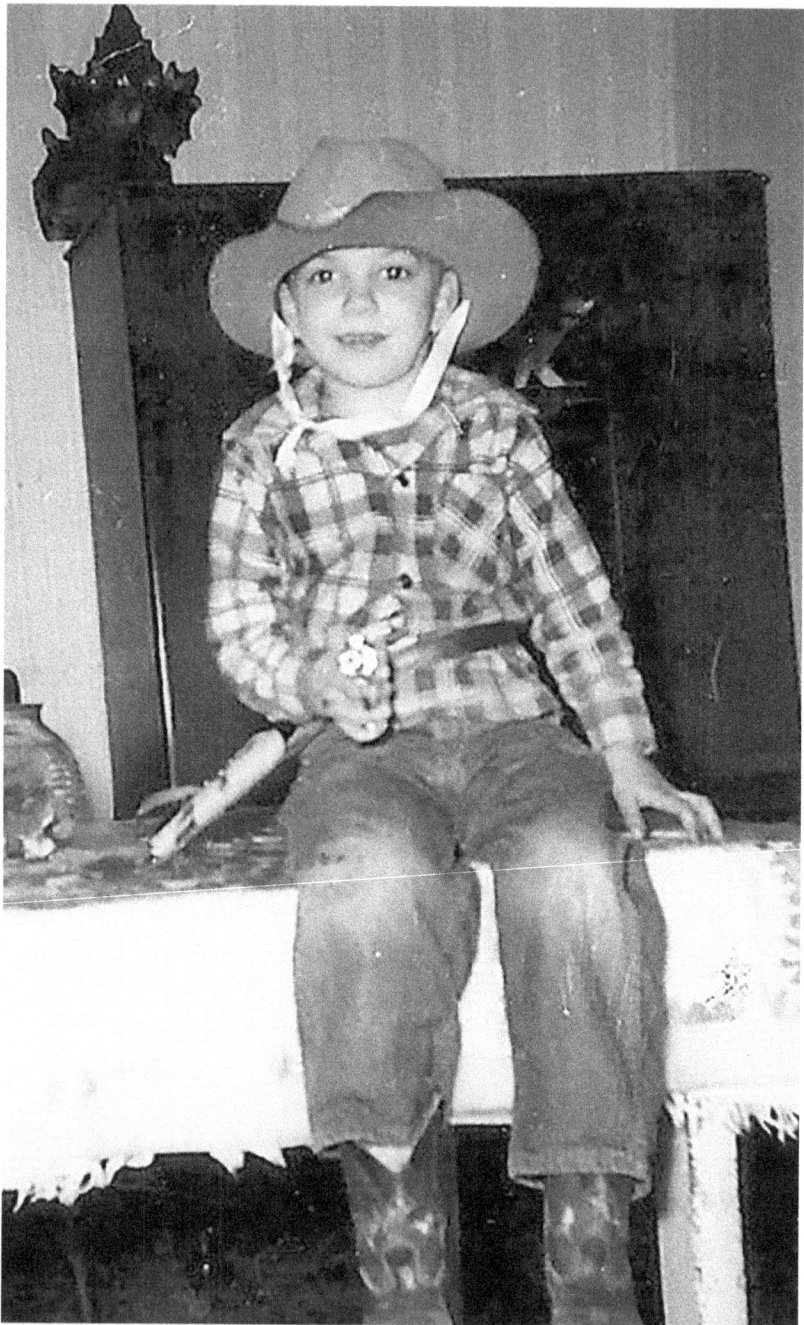

Wearing Dad Gilbert's hat, Fayetteville, AR, ca. 1951
J. B. Hogan Collection

812 York

OUR THIRD HOUSE in town was at 812 York Street. It was smaller than the other houses we had been in, but it was okay, and we were close together. We got our dog Pal there. He was a sweet black and white Australian Sheepdog. Pal was a good dog. He was loyal, my brother said, and he guarded us. He tried to bite the garbage men even when he was a little puppy.

Me and Dad Gilbert were sick at this house, too, but he let me stay with him and he played with me. He let me wear his cowboy hat, and my mother put a cloth strap on that hat so I could wear it on my head without it falling off. I got real hot at nights a lot, and my nose was stopped up, and I stretched my legs to make them stop hurting. Sometimes my mother took me to Dr. Fowler's office, or he came by our house to see Dad and me. Dr. Fowler was as tall as Dad and looked like him. They had gray hair and were old.

The road in front of our house was all dirt and was real narrow, and one day my mother took me up the hill from our house to a school. It was the first grade, and I stayed in my seat at the back of the class and didn't say anything because I didn't know any of the other kids. After that day my brother walked me up to school. Soon, I sort of got used to it at the school, and the teacher told my mom that I was doing real good. At lunch, I would walk down the street and buy a chocolate milk to eat with my bologna sandwich. It only cost two cents. The bottle of chocolate milk I mean.

The next year I was in second grade and at Christmas I got a little red wagon with a bag of oranges inside it. That was our second Christmas at that house. The first Christmas I got a little train that I pushed around a little track. In January, Dr. Fowler came by our house to see our grandpa sometimes and Dad didn't feel good. He was gray and old and his fingers were stained real yellow. He and mother smoked a lot of cigarettes.

One night after we had all gone to bed, I heard a loud noise and when I jumped up everyone was running around crying and talking loud. Dad had shot himself with one of my brother's .22 rifles. My mother was crying, and my brother whose rifle it was kept asking, "Why? Why my rifle?"

Once I peeked around the corner of the door into Dad's room and I saw my oldest brother sort of resting Dad's head on a pillow. There was a lot of blood on the pillow and around the top of Dad's body. Everyone got quiet then and my sister used our new phone to call people.

Some of our country family got there real fast, but I was taken away right about then by our next door neighbors. They were a nice couple and they came over and my sister gave me to them and they took me over to their house to spend the night. I knew Dad was going to die because I heard somebody say that before I left, but the neighbor couple never said anything about that to me and they made me some hot chocolate, and I went to sleep over at their house.

The Zion church was all full when Dad had his funeral. Everything felt funny and a lot of people were crying but not real loud. It was quiet mostly. Then they took Dad's box out to the cemetery beside the church and put it down in the ground. After that we left.

350 Combs

FTER DAD GILBERT died, we soon left the little house at 812 York Street. We moved to the south part of town, to 350 South Combs Street. People said it was the poor side of town, but we just thought it was our new house. 350 was at the end of the street where the dirt road turned to the left in front of our house.

It was a good house. It was one floor with a big living and dining and kitchen all in the front. There were two bedrooms (one for me and my two brothers and one for my mother and sister) and a screened-in back porch that we used sometimes as another bedroom.

Out front was a porch with a swing. The porch was held up by two white wood posts, the one on the right side was where I stepped on a hornet one time. That sting hurt a lot and it caused my whole left foot to swell up, and I could barely walk on the side of my foot up town to go to the movies. In back of the house there was some steps down to the back yard and an old building that had been a garage or something.

On the right side of the house was a narrow yard where I used to pull up little patches of onion grass to snack on, and on the left side was a driveway and past that, more to the left, was a big field that was our garden. There was plenty of room inside and outside for a kid like me to run and play. I liked making little roads in the dirt by

J. B. Hogan at side of house and tree, Fayetteville, AR, ca. 1954.
J. B. Hogan Collection

the driveway and then zooming my little cars around and around and making the sound of cars revving up.

Out back and on the side of our yards was a big L-shaped field that had a couple of horses in it. That field belonged to Mr. Parker. Mr. Parker's name was Otis but we all called him Mr. Parker. He was a colored man, and he was friendly. He seemed strong and proud of himself. In the spring he would bring one of his horses over and plow our garden so that we could plant carrots and corn and things. My mother said he was one of Fayetteville's better off colored people because he used to be a big cowboy. That was why his pasture and little house were located there in the white neighborhood.

Combs Street was a good place to live. Jefferson School was nearby, past Mr. Parker's field and by Buddy Hayes's house. He was a shoeshine man and he made a bunch of money doing that and because he had some kind of band. He was like Mr. Parker, a better off colored man living by us whites. Mr. Hayes was like Mr. Parker but he was funnier and laughed a lot.

I went to the rest of my second grade at Jefferson. My teacher was nice to me and asked my mother if she could give me extra work so I wouldn't be bored in class. My mother said to go ahead, and so, I got to read a lot in class and teach some of the other kids, and the teacher liked for me to read to the class because I would talk like country people and this and that when I read.

Phydella Hogan and J. B. Hogan on Bill Hogan's car, Fayetteville, AR, 1954.
J. B. Hogan Collection

All I Could Do Was Lie There Paralyzed (Sorry, Elvis)

MOST EVERY DAY when I went to school, I ducked under the barbed wire in Mr. Parker's fence, staying away from his horses, and crossed the field to a dirt road that went by Buddy Hayes's house and on over to Jefferson School. My third grade teacher was Mrs. S. She was a big lady, and I don't think she liked me much. She wasn't nice like my second grade teacher.

One morning I was going to school and when I ducked under the barbed wire fence in Mr. Parker's field I felt a real sharp sting on top of my head. I felt under my Cub Scout cap and there was blood all on my hands. I went back home, and my mother called a cab and we went to a doctor. He wasn't Dr. Fowler, I don't know why. He asked if I had had a tetanus shot and then he gave me what he called a booster shot. We came home after that and I went on to school.

After lunch, my legs started feeling funny, all tingly and stuff. They felt funny and I moved them around and sat on them because it made the tingle stop a little. I kept doing that in class and finally Mrs. S. got mad at me or something and she came over and said, "Little mister, you stop that wiggling around."

I didn't say anything because I was afraid of her and because my mother had told me not to ever sass a teacher. But my legs kept feeling funny and I kept squirming around when Mrs. S. wasn't looking.

She caught me though, sure enough, caught me sitting on my legs again trying to get the tingling to stop.

"All right, buster." Mrs. S. grabbed me by the arm and pulled me up out of the seat and swatted my butt two or three times. It didn't hurt much and I didn't cry but the class laughed at me. Everybody thought that was funny, me being spanked and all.

After school, I went straight home and laid down on my bed. I didn't eat much for supper and then I went to bed early. Nobody seemed to notice that much because I was sick a lot of the time anyway. My legs kept feeling funnier and funnier, but I fell asleep and slept all night, anyway.

In the morning, I woke up and felt fine, except when I started to get out of bed I couldn't move my legs. They didn't have any feeling in them at all. Neither one of them. I made one more try and then I hollered for my mother. My big brother Bill got to me first because he was right there in the room.

"Mom," he screamed, "Jerry's paralyzed. He can't feel his legs. He's paralyzed. He can't move."

My mom and my other brother Joe and my sister Martha all started talking and yelling and my big brother carried me outside to his car, a 1939 four-door Chevy, it was real neat. Bill and Mother took me back to the doctor and he checked me over and explained to us that I must've had a tetanus shot not too long ago because I was having a reaction to the shot. He smiled and said I would be okay when the medicine wore off and for us not to worry. I could skip school today and rest, I liked that, and I'd be fine soon.

On the way home, Bill and my mom seemed a lot more relaxed than they were before and I wasn't scared anymore myself. I had a great day lying around in bed and got my food and stuff brought to me. It was real neat and I enjoyed myself. The feeling came back into my legs by about lunchtime, but I didn't let on I was completely okay until I was sure I would get to skip school for the whole day.

The next morning I felt okay. My legs weren't numb anymore and I could walk fine. I sort of tried to act like I maybe should stay home another day and rest some more, but my mother had me get dressed and go on to school. My legs were all right and so was I.

Be prepared! J. B. Hogan as a Cub Scout, c. 1954.
J. B. Hogan Collection

A Tree or a Monkey, Betsy Ross, and the Wizard of Oz

CUB SCOUTS WAS fun when you got done doing the things you were supposed to do to get badges and stuff. The Den Mother always gave you cookies and milk and things like that. Sometimes my mother was the Den Mother. The bad thing some other times was that they had these plays and everybody was supposed to be in them. The first one I was in I was a tree or a monkey or something like that. I felt dumb and stood at the back of the stage not doing anything.

Worse than the tree or monkey was the next play. They made me play Betsy Ross. I had to play Betsy Ross because I was the only boy who knew how to use a needle and thread. My mother taught all us boys that. "All boys need to know how to sew socks and buttons, and they need to know how to cook a little and how to iron some clothes and keep their place clean. You'll be independent that way." Bill was going into the Air Force soon and she had already taught him those things. "You can always use these skills. Boys need to know how to take care of themselves, too."

I still didn't want to be Betsy Ross even if my being independent was why I was gonna be. But they made me. I had to sit in a stupid chair with a stupid dress on and pretend to be sewing this stupid flag. I felt really dumb. I felt like an idiot. An idiot, that was what I heard Bill call this guy he got in a fight with one time. I knew what an idiot was now.

That play got over, at last, but I was hating thinking of the next one. I couldn't imagine how bad it would be. First a tree or a monkey and then Betsy Ross, I was thinking maybe of quitting the Cub Scouts. Ha, but I was wrong. I got a good one. My mother said it was my reward for not squawking about being Betsy Ross. I got to play the Wizard of Oz in our next play. The Wizard himself. I was a big shot. I was the star of the show.

I did okay except in this one part where I was supposed to pop a balloon one boy was wearing as a head. My mother had filled the balloon up with cigarette smoke and I was supposed to have a pin and pop the balloon and the smoke would all come out. When it came to that part, I didn't have a pin. I didn't know what to do, so I started beating the tar out of that balloon. I probably bopped the kid on the head a bunch, too. The audience was laughing, but we went on with it, and later everyone said I did okay as the Wizard. That made the whole play thing okay. It started bad, but it ended good. I was happy with that.

Cheese, Crackers,
and a Cute Girlfriend

MY FOURTH GRADE teacher was Mrs. McCandless. She wasn't like Mrs. S. at all. I liked Mrs. McCandless. It was fun to be in her class. Every afternoon we had a rest time, and we got cheese and crackers. She chose me to go get the crackers. That was important. She could trust me, she said.

So when we had our cheese and crackers before we rested, Mrs. McCandless gave me some money, and I left school, walking downstairs to the big doors and going outside all by myself and went up the street past Jefferson School to the corner. I had to stop at the corner and look in both directions before I went across the street to the little store where I bought the crackers.

Mr. and Mrs. Johnson owned the store, and they always smiled at me and told me I must be a dependable boy that the teacher would trust me to get the crackers. I would hide my face and give them the money, and they would give me the crackers and some change back, and I would take it all back to class, and we would all have our cheese and crackers and then take a rest.

Other times we would do class stuff and I sat by this girl named Melinda. She was pretty and had dark hair and smiled at me and even talked to me. She was my girlfriend, and when we went on class things away from school we would always ride on the bus beside

Jefferson Elementary School, Fayetteville, AR.
Photo by J. B. Hogan

each other and then walk together during the trip and come back to school together. Sometimes looking at her made me sigh.

My friend Jimmy liked her, too, and sometimes she would go with him on stuff. Sometimes she would go with both of us on stuff, too. Sometimes me and Jimmy would sort of push each other to get next to her or try to trick the other one so that one of us could get beside Melinda. I liked her a lot, but Jimmy did too and we both tried to be her boyfriend. She was my girlfriend but sometimes she was Jimmy's girlfriend, too. I tried to make her my girlfriend more than she was Jimmy's. I did okay most of the time. She was real cute. She had dark hair and she smiled at me a lot.

Somebody Ought to Be Crying

WHEN MY SISTER was to get married, my mother decided we should have the wedding right there in our house on Combs Street. All the furniture got moved around, and we set up chairs so that everyone was looking up toward the front of the house where the preacher was and where my sister and her boyfriend were going to get married.

My cousin Larry and his family came in from the country for the wedding and because me and him were thick as thieves we sat beside each other in a couple of those fold-up chairs that you see in the back of churches and gyms and stuff. We were sitting there together kind of whispering and giggling at all the fancy stuff going on and the clothes people were wearing. My mom wagged her finger at us a couple of times, and we tried to settle down, but it was hard to do. When we was together, me and Larry always acted up. We had fun.

Somewhere in there where the wedding was going along, Larry had this idea come to him. He leaned over to me and whispered.

"You know what this wedding needs?"

"What?" I figured it was something good. Larry always had good ideas, even if they sometimes got us in trouble with our moms or his dad. "What does it need?"

"You notice something missing?" He had a funny look on his face.

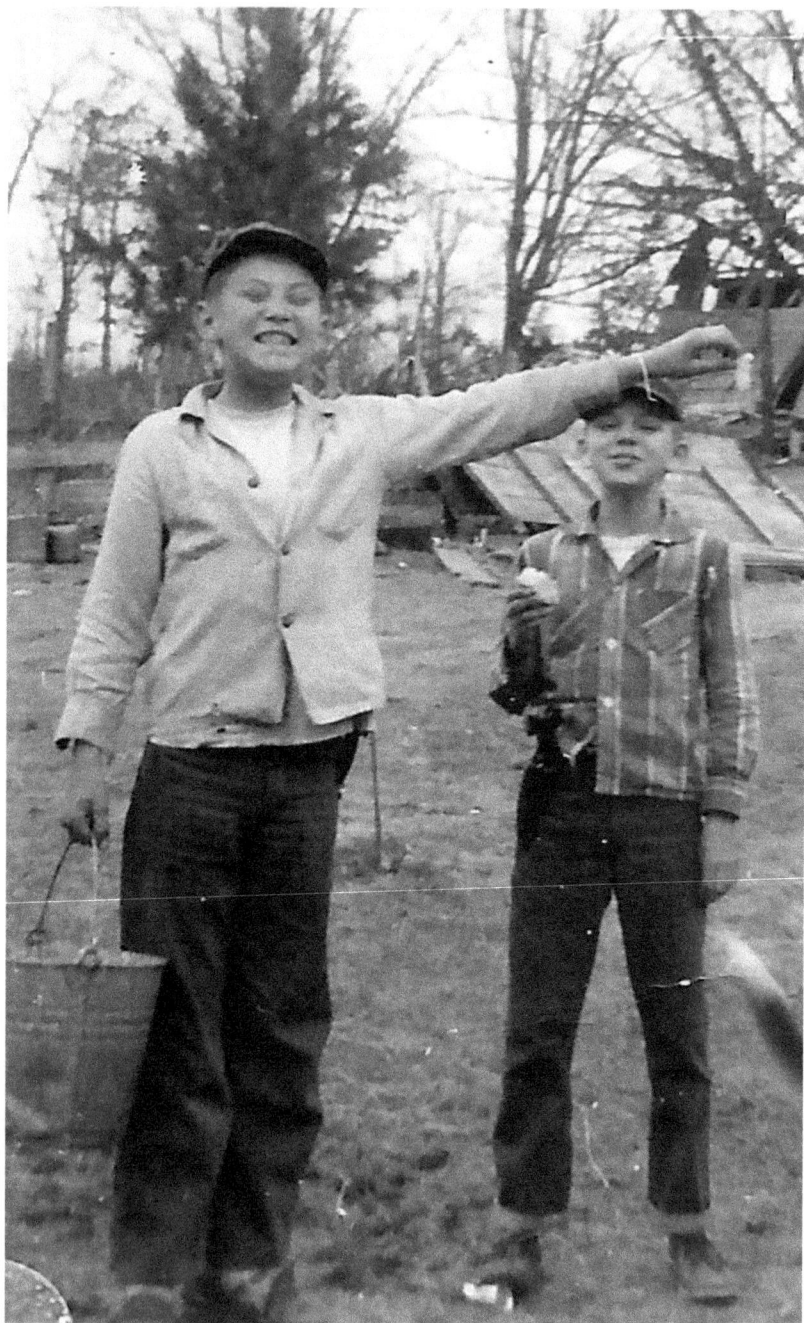

Larry Fultz, left, and J. B. Hogan, Mayfield, AR, 1957.
J. B. Hogan Collection

"Missing?"

"They ain't nobody crying." He snickered.

I looked around at all the people. Nobody was crying.

"They're not. They're not crying."

"Somebody ought to be crying." It sounded reasonable to me, at least the way he said it and all.

"I reckon." I agreed, knowing we were probably gonna get it for this one.

"That's what's missing." He giggled. I giggled, too.

He made some kind of sign so that I knew it was time for us to start crying. Without thinking about nothing we leaned back and started wailing. It was close to what people use to call caterwauling. We were laughing out loud in between fake sobbing and crying. But our little crying jag didn't last long. Not too long at all. Because before we'd got more than a strong wail or two out, my mother came running at us as fast and as mad as you can imagine. She was coming right for us. We tried to get out another big cry, but she was on us.

"You boys stop that, right now." She sounded real tough-like, not her usual way.

I could tell she wasn't fooling around. I shut up fast. Larry kept laughing for a second or two until he realized mom was madder'n a hornet at us.

"Stop acting like a couple of howling banshees. You boys behave this instant, or I'll paddle both your butts in front of everybody. And good, too. I'll give you something to cry about."

I started to say something, but the look on her face was real rough, and I hung my head and stared at my shiny shoes. Before me or Larry could do or say anything else, she grabbed us both by the shirt collars and pulled us right up out of our chairs even though she wasn't much bigger than Larry was. Next thing you know, she pushes me and him into my bedroom and sits us down in there.

"Now, you two stay in here until the service is over and don't you dare make so much as a hint of a whimper, you understand?" She wasn't smiling. We understood.

We stayed in the bedroom until the wedding service part was over. We sat there and were real quiet. We didn't laugh much and we sure didn't do any more fake crying. That would have gotten our rear ends tanned for sure. We knew when to stop. We knew better'n to push it too much with mom. She was little, but she could spank you hard, and worse than that, she could give you a chewing out that made you feel worse than any whipping ever could.

When the service was over, she came and got us out of the bedroom and let us rejoin everybody out in the big main room where we had cake and punch and stuff like that. She didn't seem mad at us anymore, and nobody said anything about the fake crying.

Me and Larry figured we got off easy. We didn't get a spanking, and we got to have treats after the wedding, anyway. We had learned our lesson about fake crying at a wedding, though. But that was only one lesson. There was lots more stuff you could do to have fun in life and lots more lessons to learn. One lesson learned never stopped us from trying something different at another time. It never had and it never would.

Who You Callin' Poor?

WHEN WE HAD been on Combs Street for a while was the first time I heard that we were supposed to be poor. My mom went to get us some government help but the lady at the office must've said something mean to her because I heard my mother say she would never ask for any help again.

It didn't seem to matter much whether somebody helped us or not. We always had food, and my mom was a terrific cook, and she made us good meals all the time when she was not working.

We ate beans and cornbread, biscuits and gravy sometimes with little thin minute steaks, bacon and eggs, blackberry cobbler, chocolate chip cookies, and on Friday, we had salmon croquettes. That food tasted wonderful. Nobody said anything about that being poor people's food.

Mother worked mostly at night then, her and my oldest brother. They made almost all the money we had by working at a drive-in restaurant down on Dickson Street. When my brother wasn't working down there at the drive-in, he was on the Boys Club boxing team. He was good and tough. He used to smile, it said in the paper, when the guy he was fighting hit him a hard one. Then he would beat the tar out of the other guy, usually.

After a fight, he would come home, and if we hadn't gone to the fight and he'd won, he would come into the house all down in the dumps acting and we'd all go, "Ah, you lost, that's too bad." And then he'd suddenly smile real big and laugh and grab me or somebody and swing us around and then holler out about him winning the fight. That was always fun when he won a fight and did that fake losing thing. We got a kick out of that.

Christmases were fun at Combs Street, too, because we had this fat little Santa Claus that we could plug in, and he had a light in him that glowed. We had silver icicles and popcorn strings and bulb ornaments. The bulbs were green and red and gold, and I would stare at them, and they would make me feel happy and good. We also had these plastic or something icicles and you could hold them up to a light and then put them on the tree and turn all the lights out and the icicles would glow for quite a while. We liked that a lot.

One year we gave ourselves a present of a record player that had a radio in it. Man, that was something. We could listen to the news and listen to ball games and play this bunch of old 78 records that were in the house and some 45s, too. It was our best family present ever.

One summer, right when it started getting warm, my oldest brother went away. He joined the Air Force. Later in the year was my sister's marriage and she moved to over by Tulsa. My other brother started working all the time then, and I was alone almost all the time in our house, except for early in the morning and late at night.

I liked being alone after a while. I got used to the house being empty and quiet and saw that there wasn't any ghosts or anything in it to get me when no one else was there. I listened to the radio and played civil war games and played with my little tinker toy set and made up my own games. I had fun most of the time.

The best part about it was that in the evening, when I was there at the house all by myself, one of the delivery guys from the drive-in where my mother, and now my other brother, worked all the time would bring me my supper when he had a delivery not too far from our house. That was great. I could get a hamburger deluxe, the one with tomatoes and lettuce, or even a cheeseburger deluxe, French fries, and a coke or a milk shake, and it was all delivered to me there at my house all by myself.

I heard some guy say one time to my mother, "Heck, that ain't poor. I don't see anybody else getting his meals delivered to him like he was a king or something. Don't sound poor to me. Sounds like he's being spoiled rotten, if you ask me."

That made sense to me, too, I guess, so I wasn't mad about not being considered poor. Only thing I didn't like was that part about being spoiled rotten. I didn't like that. I didn't know what I'd been doing to make him think I was spoiled rotten. Shoot, I was hanging around my house, doing my schoolwork and playing games by my-self. I got my food from the drive-in every night. My momma was responsible for that anyway not that delivery guy.

Maybe I was poor and maybe I wasn't, I didn't know anything about that, but I never could see how getting to eat supper like every-body else was supposed to make me spoiled rotten. No, sir, I never did understand that. I don't think that delivery guy knew so much, even if he was a grownup.

J. B. Hogan, kneeling, eating ice cream, Fayetteville, AR, 1955.
J. B. Hogan Collection

Don't Break Wind
and the 8:10 Train

THE OLD GUY whose house we lived in for a month or two before we moved to Hill Street had been a policeman or something, and he was weird. If me or my brother cut a fart and he heard it, he would always chew us out and say, "Don't break wind." When he wasn't there or we were outside, we would fart or act like it and then yell at each other, "Don't break wind." That made us laugh. That old guy was weird.

His house was about ten feet, I swear, from the railroad track. At least the back of the tiny back yard was. Man, when the 8:10 train came rumbling by at night, the whole house shook, and the train whistle would wake the dead from that close. You couldn't hear a single thing until that train was gone, and we were usually listening to the radio about then, a Yankees game maybe or on Wednesday or Friday nights, the fights.

We didn't stay long in that old man's house. That was good. We were glad to get the heck out of there.

A Couple of Cowboys, Some Students, and One Strange Lodger

THE HOUSE AT 112 South Hill Street was really big. It was two stories tall with a stairway going up to the second floor in front of you to the right when you came in the front door. There was a small living room to the left downstairs and then on down the hall on the left was the kitchen with the dinner table and chairs. On the right by the front door was another room and then a big room, that was me and my brother's room, and a little room in back where our mother slept. There were big windows all around the house, including one by my room that I shattered one time when I hit a line drive from out in the yard. My mother didn't like that but she didn't punish me.

She did tell me over and over to stop bouncing balls off the walls inside the house. So what I did was put my football helmet, it didn't have a face mask, on the living room couch and surround it with pillows so that I could run around the room with a baseball and shoot the ball at the helmet like I was playing basketball. I always made the final shot that allowed the Razorbacks to the win the game. If I missed, I took the shot again until I made it and we won.

The upstairs part of our house had four or five rooms, too, and my mom decided to rent those out and make our house a room and board place. I liked most of the guys who came to live at our house upstairs. There was a cowboy and a truck driver and one cool college student guy and one sort of uncool college student guy but he did record our mother and her family playing music.

My mother played the banjo, and my aunt played the banjo and guitar and sang. This college guy I didn't like much took a tape recorder out to my aunt's and recorded them and one of my cousins playing music. That was kind of neat, even if he wasn't.

All these guys ate breakfast with us in the morning and supper with us at night and that was part of their room and board at the big house. The cowboy and the truck driver had a lot of funny stories, and my brother used to hang out with them, but my mother didn't like that too much so he had to kind of sneak around with them. When they got back he was always chewing a lot of gum because he'd been smoking and drinking beer. Our mother would've killed him if she'd caught him drinking.

One night close to Christmas, a weird thing happened. Me and my brother and my mother were sitting around the kitchen table when there was a knock at the front door. It was late for somebody to be coming around knocking on the door. We all went to see who it was and it was this kind of hobo=looking guy standing on the porch. Mom switched on the front porch light and the guy squinted into the light.

"Good evening, ma'am." He took off his ragged cloth hat. He had dark stubble on his face like he hadn't shaved in a while and his clothes were old and kind of shiny from being dirty.

"Good evening."

"I understand that this is a rooming house?"

"We're a room and board, sir," she said. "We usually rent by the week or month."

"I see."

He kind of shuffled around and seemed to be cold. It was cold on us standing there with the front door wide open. Me and my brother glanced over at our mom. She looked at us and then at the man again.

"We do have one small room upstairs in the back that's open right now." She smiled. "I don't see why you couldn't take it for the night, right boys?"

"That's right, mom." Me and my brother agreed enthusiastically. The hobo guy didn't look like a bad man at all. He seemed real nice.

"That would be truly kind of you, ma'am, but I doubt that I have even enough…."

"Never mind, you come in out of the cold and rest for one night. It won't hurt anything."

"Thank you kindly." He sort of bowed toward mom.

"You boys show the gentleman the room upstairs."

"Yes, ma'am."

After we settled the guy in the little room at the back of the landing upstairs, me and my brother hustled down to our mother.

"Who do you think he is?" I wanted to know. "A tramp? A hobo?"

"Maybe he's an escaped criminal," my brother suggested.

"He's most likely just a man down on his luck, boys. Don't worry about him."

But me and my brother kept talking about him after we went back to our room across the hall from the kitchen.

"Who do you think he is?" I asked again.

"A bum probably."

"He seemed awful nice to be a bum."

"Maybe."

"What if he's Jesus testing us." I blurted it out. I think I had been reading the Bible lately and the idea popped into my head.

"Why would Jesus come here?" My brother sort of laughed.

"He would come here to test us." I reasoned. "To see if we were like the Good Samaritan, you know, if we would be kind to a complete stranger."

"That's pretty farfetched."

"You can't ever tell. It might be him"

"It might be."

Not too long before bedtime, mom came over to our room.

"Would you boys like to take that man in the little room some food before you go to bed?"

"Hot dog!" I exclaimed. "You bet."

"Sure, mom."

Upstairs, we knocked softly on the man's door. He opened the door, still dressed exactly like he had been out on the front porch except he had put his hat on a little table by his small bed.

"Hi, boys."

"Good evening, sir." My brother spoke for us. "Our mom thought you might like something to eat before going to bed."

"God bless you." The man took the plate my brother held out.

Mom had made him a ham and cheese sandwich and put a couple of chocolate chip cookies on the side. I came out from behind my brother where I'd been hiding and gave the man a cup of hot coffee.

"And God bless your mother." The man smiled at me. "How kind you all are."

"Good night, sir."

"Good night, boys. Thank you again."

We closed the door behind us and, with a little squeal, I chased after my brother down the stairs. We ran to tell mom we'd delivered the food to the man.

"Thank you boys, now you get to bed. It's getting late."

"Yes, mom." We headed off to our bedroom.

It wasn't easy to go to sleep that night, at least for me. I kept thinking about who that man might be. Could he be Jesus? Was he a tramp or a hobo? A man down on his luck like our mom said. Finally, after a long time I fell asleep.

"Get up, squirt." My brother called to me early the next morning. We still had some school left before the holiday and had to get up and go.

Out in the kitchen, mom had made a big old breakfast for everybody and we took turns sitting at the table eating bacon and eggs and toast. The others had coffee, but I drank hot chocolate. For some reason I had completely forgotten about the man who'd come in the night before and didn't remember him until me and my brother were heading down the hallway toward the front door to go to school.

"You suppose the man is still up there?" I asked as we got to the bottom of the stairs by the door.

"I don't know… look here."

He pointed at the top of the post on the bottom of the stairs. It was an envelope, taped onto the post.

"What's that?"

"Look and see."

I unstuck the envelope and opened it. Inside was a small piece of paper with the words *"Thank you"* scribbled in pencil. Digging around, I found thirty-seven cents in change. It had to come from the strange hobo man. Me and my brother raced upstairs and sure enough he had already got up and gone.

He was nowhere to be seen.

We brought his plate and cup down and went out on the porch to look around in case he was still somewhere nearby but he wasn't. He was long gone. We showed our mother the envelope with the note and the thirty-seven cents in it. She smiled and shook her head.

"It was what he could afford. Probably almost all he had."

"We were like Good Samaritans." I was proud, recalling my Sunday school lesson.

"No, *he* was, boys. He was more the Good Samaritan than we were."

Me and my brother didn't exactly get it. Our mother seemed to understand, though. We shrugged our shoulders, and headed back out into the hallway. It was getting late and we had to get to school on time. Outside it was clear and cold, but it would be warm and comfortable in the school. We hurried along our way.

Ether, Ether and No Sense of Smell (They Could Have At Least Left My Adenoids In)

I WAS SICK my entire sixth grade year. I missed over half of the school days. That made me have to go to summer school. But right before summer, Dr. Fowler decided that my tonsils were ready to be taken out and that might make me feel better.

The hospital room was cool and clean, and I felt nervous. But they gave me a shot of something and I felt good. I saw baseball players playing a game on the wall across from my bed. That made me laugh. Then they took me in to get my tonsils out. The doctor leaned over me and smiled. I was kind of scared.

"Count back from one hundred." The doctor hooked up this cloth thing over my nose and mouth. "The ether will make you go to sleep. Next thing you know, you'll be awake again."

"One hundred, ninety-nine, ninety… eight, ni… ne… ty… sev…." That was as far as I got. It got all black, completely.

The next thing I knew I was down in this deep black place with a bright light above me somewhere and I was fighting, struggling, to get to that bright light. There was a strong smell like when you stand right behind a city bus and it takes off with the exhaust air hitting you right in the nose. It made me want to throw up.

I woke up kind of fighting for my breath and feeling bad. My head hurt and my throat was sore, and I couldn't get that bad smell out of my nose. It wouldn't go away. I wondered where I had been. It felt like I had died or something and then barely made it back to life. I was scared.

After a while, I began to feel better but I noticed that I was sore in back of my nose, too, not only in the throat. The doctors said I could have all the ice cream I wanted but I didn't want much ice cream. I felt too much like throwing up all the time.

In a day or so, I got to go home. I felt a lot better by then. My head didn't hurt much anymore and the soreness behind my nose had gotten better. I thought my throat was getting well, too, and when my mom I wanted to know what I wanted to eat, I asked for biscuits and gravy. She made them for me but when I took a big old bite I let out a scream. The biscuits felt like they scraped my throat clean out. I cried like a baby and my mom apologized but it wasn't her fault it was the biscuits' fault. After that I only drank liquid stuff for a couple of days and then I was all right.

I got well after that. I didn't hardly ever miss school again and I didn't get those strep throat things and stuff like that. Only a cold or a flu sometimes. It was wonderful. I finally felt good. I knew I was healthy now. I got to play all the sports again with no problem and I even got attendance awards in the eighth grade.

The only thing left over from taking out my tonsils and my adenoids, the doctor said he took them out, too, while he was in there, was for a long time I couldn't bear to be too close to a bus when it started up. The bus exhaust was like the ether to me and that was scary and sickening like when I felt as if I'd died during the operation.

The other thing was, I couldn't smell much stuff anymore. I couldn't smell flowers and things like that. I couldn't even smell farts or dead skunks. That was funny because some things I could smell, like a lady's strong perfume, or some foods cooking, or bus exhaust. I never knew what I would smell or what I wouldn't. It was sort of hit or miss, mostly miss.

But I wasn't sick anymore. I was well. I was healthy. I didn't mind trading most of the things that other people could smell for that. Nope, I'd take feeling good over smelling things any time, no doubt about it.

J. B. Hogan, Fayetteville, AR, 1957-1958.
J. B. Hogan Collection

In a Junior High Daze

IN THE SEVENTH grade I did okay with my grades. But most of the time I kind of felt odd and awkward like I didn't belong inside my own body. I wore an old Yankees hat I had ordered from Manny's in New York City. I found the ad in the back of Street and Smith's 1955 baseball guide book and sent off for the hat. I never took it off from the fifth grade through the sixth.

Right away in seventh grade, my homeroom teacher took me aside and suggested that I probably would want to stop wearing the Yankees hat all the time. I understood her to mean that girls wouldn't think the hat was a cool thing for a guy to be wearing constantly. I stopped wearing the hat so much, but it didn't help me with the girls. None of them thought I was cool, anyway.

What I did at school was mostly wait for lunch hour so I could shoot marbles in the dirt off to the side of the asphalt playground with some of the other guys. Or flatten out one of those small milk cartons you get in the cafeteria and then me and my buddy Rodney would play one on one football trying to see who could get past the other one and score a TD. Rodney was fastern' heck and so it was good practice. Doing that made me a better football player, especially in the eighth grade when I played in an after school tackle league for mostly the smaller guys who couldn't play on bigger teams. I did well at that.

The main thing that ever happened when I was in junior high happened when I was in the eighth grade. There were these two big guys in the ninth grade. One was a good guy, an athlete, a solid student. The other guy was a bad guy, he was a hood, and he was tough as heck and scared us little guys half to death.

One day in the spring these two guys started having a big argument out by the playground fence. They were off the asphalt in some scraggly grass yelling at each other. I didn't get close enough to find out what they were yelling back and forth but it was scary to see and hear even from a distance. These guys were big and had big muscles.

"They gonna duke it out." Rodney and me halted our milk carton football game to watch the big guys go at each other.

"Why are they fighting?"

"I don't know but I think it was about some girl."

"Oh." I wondered about that. I had never had a girl like me hardly at all, except for my fourth grade girlfriend, and I sure couldn't imagine getting in a fight with one of those guys over a girl. Guys like that would beat the tar out of you.

"Look out." Rodney whistled, pointed over at the two big guys.

They had suddenly started pushing one another and they were snarling and snapping at each other like big, mean dogs or something. Then the bad big guy swung at the good big guy and the fight was on. Man, it was something to watch. They grabbed each other and flung each other around. I remember them crashing into the playground fence and it bowed out and kinda bent at the bottom. They were big, strong guys.

After the wrestling around, the two guys started punching each other. Whew, they hit hard. You could hear the smacks all the way across the asphalt playground.

"Holy cow." The fight seemed like one of those gigantic duke outs like I had been reading about in my Greek Mythology book in my English class. I mean it was a big fight.

The two guys hit each other three or four times each and then the good big guy popped the bad big guy right in the face. Pop. The bad guy fell to his knees holding onto a link in the chain fence. He tried to get up but the good guy hit him again real hard and the bad guy went back down to his knees.

The good guy said something that I couldn't hear then and the bad guy waved him off like the fight was over. He didn't want any more. It was amazing. The good guy won the fight. Several people crowded around the winner guy, and they walked away from the bad guy who was left there on his knees with only one guy and a girl standing beside him. I was bowled over by the whole thing.

What was even more amazing was that old Mo, as we called him, the tobacco-chewing, paddle-carrying and rear-end busting principal of the school, never even came out during this fight and neither the good guy or the bad guy ever got in trouble for that big fight. Shoot, old Mo paddled my butt for nothing more than leaning my foot on a big metal cable that was strung between two wooden posts to keep cars out, I guess, from the playground.

Old Mo was meaner'n heck to everybody. But he never even came out during that big fight. Maybe it was because it turned out the way he wanted it to. You know, what with the good guy winning and all. We never knew for sure. What we did know was that it was the biggest fight anyone had ever seen so far in their lives. It was something you wouldn't forget. I knew I never would anyway.

J. B. Hogan, Calipatria, CA, 1962.
J. B. Hogan Collection

The Incredible Shrinking Boy and California Movin'

WHEN YOU'RE PHYSICALLY small, even if you're an okay athlete, this is what happens to you in a medium to large high school. It's like that 1950s movie *The Incredible Shrinking Man*. A cloud seems to appear from out of nowhere, passes quietly over you, and leaves you unchanged except for one minor detail.

You begin to shrink, imperceptibly at first, then quicker, faster, until those around you, who could barely see you to begin with, no longer notice your existence. You're there, but you're not there. You exist, but you don't exist. You are nothing, smaller than the infinitesimal, left on your own to fight giant spiders, eat tiny chunks of moldy cheese, walk through the little individual squares of screen wire.

Well, it's not quite that bad, but when you are a small, uncool, basically shy and unhip kind of guy, you do tend to be overlooked by your classmates. By the end of my sophomore year, I had become so invisible that I didn't even make it past the first cut for the high school baseball team. Baseball, my sport, my love, my only salvation from a life of meaninglessness. Didn't even get a second look. I had a couple of good friends in my life and that was about it. Some of my teachers noticed me, mostly my English teacher. None of the girls did. I was a loser, heading toward permanent loser-land. Then I got lucky.

———————————

A S EARLY AS my sixth grade, my mother had been considering moving out to California for her health. After raising us four kids, almost completely by herself, she did get some occasional help, but not much, she had begun to come a little unraveled emotionally and physically. We didn't go to California then, but after my middle brother went into the Air Force in 1958, leaving just my mother and me, she started seriously thinking about moving away.

In March of 1961, toward the end of my sophomore year, she bolted for the Imperial Valley of California where her sister and husband, my aunt and uncle, and other of our relatives lived. They had gone there at the end of the Great Depression in order to find work.

As soon as my semester was over, I hopped a bus and headed for California to join my mother. I left everything I knew behind, family, friends, Fayetteville—my beautiful Ozark Mountain hometown. The moment I climbed on board that bus, it was like a wall came down behind me. The past was instantly gone. The present and the future were all that existed.

My Uncle Alec picked me up at the El Centro bus station, after the long bus ride, to take me to my new home in Calipatria, thirty miles north in this desert, farming valley. I still remember that drive in his open-air jeep. It was early evening but still hot and more humid than I expected. I knew nothing yet about the Imperial Valley and its massive, ubiquitous irrigation system. As we drove north, I remember how the palm trees lining the streets of Imperial, the county seat, seemed so exciting and exotic to me.

I was greeted by my mother and aunt as the long lost prodigal son when my uncle and I arrived at their little wood house on the west side of Calipatria. After eating bus station food for two or three days, my aunt's hamburgers, with her mixture of mayonnaise and mustard on the buns, were about as tasty as any food I'd ever had. I was glad to be back with my mother and to get to know my California family. The valley may have been new to me, but I was predisposed to like it and I did.

It Is Hotter Than Hades in the Imperial Valley

YOU KNOW THAT old expression, of course, but in the case of the Imperial Valley it's literally true. The heat comes at you from mid-May to the end of September without relief. 115 to 120 degrees is common. I found this out right away.

When I first got there, my uncle took us all, me, my mom, and my aunt that is, out to the sand dunes near my new hometown. I loved the dunes. They were beautiful and tall and clean looking. I ran down one dune and started up the next. That was as far as I got. I stopped halfway up. I could barely breathe and I thought I was going to have heat stroke. I slowly walked back down that dune, my feet going deep in the sand, and even slower back up the one to my uncle's Jeep. I did try to act like everything was cool, reverse pun intended.

One afternoon later in the summer while I was staying at my cousin Walter's farm outside of town, out of boredom I decided to go jump on his kids' trampoline for a while, wrong! I jumped about three or four times and stopped. I sat down on the trampoline and slowly climbed back down onto the burning sandy ground that passed for some Platonic version of a side yard. You know, the mere projection of something grander and better, like a real yard.

I wobbled over to a thermometer nailed to the side of the house. It read 126 degrees, Fahrenheit. It could have been in the sun. It didn't matter. I went back into the house. Even swamp cooling was way superior to being outside. I poured a coke into a tall glass full of ice cubes and held it against my face before drinking. That was all the trampoline action I required for the time being, thank you.

I have lots more stories about the Imperial Valley heat but I won't go into them. They're merely different versions of the two stories above. Trust me on that one.

J. B. Hogan in high school football uniform, Calipatria, CA, 1962.
J. B. Hogan Collection

If There Are Only 49 Kids in Your Class, You Have a Shot at Doing All Right

ONE THING ABOUT going to a tiny school is that if you can walk upright without falling over at inopportune times, you get to play all the sports. It's great. You can play football, basketball, baseball, whatever. You get the chance not only to play on those teams but to start on them, to even have a chance to do well if you get lucky.

You can date cheerleaders, you can be king of a prom, you can do and be all the things that going to a larger school completely eliminates for you. Remember, if you're a small duck in real life, in a small pond you can still be a big duck. It's a wonderful feeling, and I'll never forget it or the opportunity to get to do it. Thanks, small town America.

Was I Going to Be a Professional Dishwasher?

AFTER FOOTBALL SEASON was over in my junior year, I had to get some kind of job in order to buy my own clothes, have some spending money, and maybe help my mother out at least a little bit with the household expenses. Not much on the latter, I admit, but some. What was I going to do?

I had worked the last month of my first summer in California for my cousin Walter cleaning, sanding, and repainting all the school buses at our high school, but that was a one time job. I had to come up with something that would last longer and that I could work at during the school year. What would the job be? Well, it would be my old standby, dishwasher.

Oh, yeah, dishwasher. Now, that's a wonderful job. Hotter'n heck all night long, sweaty, greasy, lowest totem on the pole, get me this, get me that. Hey, it was a job. And it was practically the only thing I was qualified to do. When I started dishwashing late in the fall of my junior year, I was merely resuming the professional career that life seemed to have carved out for me several years before.

I remember it all vividly. On, or near, my twelfth birthday, my mother marched me uptown to some government office and got me my own social security number. You betcha, gotta have one of those babies if you're going to work in these United States, pal. And don't be worrying about child labor laws. In 1957 in the south, it wasn't all that unusual to be starting your work life at twelve, or even younger.

I'd had it soft up until then. I knew that because older guys would say that sort of thing back then and I knew they knew the score. And I did know I had it soft. My mother had allowed me to do kind of whatever I pleased up to this point, not counting a few household chores and an occasional small job that might have earned me fifty cents or so. I suspect she went easy on me not because I was the baby of the family, and babies always get every break possible, but because she had to leave me alone so much of the time and I hadn't caused any problems for her, other than inappropriately wailing at weddings and such.

My first dishwashing job was at the Fayetteville Bus Station. I got the job somewhere around the holiday season in the middle of the seventh grade. I was paid twenty-five cents an hour and although the work wasn't so hard, mostly hot and greasy, I hated it and resented it and could barely stand it. If you've ever worked in a restaurant in any capacity you know what the "rush" is. It's that time when everybody comes in to eat and you are busier than a one-legged man in a butt kicking contest.

Anyway, I didn't last long at the bus station. I think I managed to whine enough to get myself either let go or my mother pitied me and let me off the hook. Either way I acted badly, I'm sure of that. Which brings me to a separate point. Never, not once, in my life have I liked a job I had, well, with the exception of teaching at the university level, but that's another story altogether.

So, after my first pathetic entry into the working class world of the dishwasher, I was luckily unemployed again. But not for too long.

My mother, for a tiny little country person with only an eighth grade education and not many working skills to speak of, had an ambitious streak in her. So, sometime during 1958, she decided to leave her job at Jug Wheeler's Drive-In in Fayetteville and open up her own café. It was a fly by the seat of your pants operation, and I don't think it ever had much of a chance of success, although the food was good, the place was, naturally for my mother, clean as a whistle, and we did have a small, cadre of loyal University of Arkansas students, mostly foreigners.

I worked for my mother irregularly. She paid me thirty-five cents an hour, up a dime from the bus station, and put up with my sports playing and goofing off with friends, both of which activities tended to make me a poor employee. The café failed after a few months, not from my mother's lack of trying, and in retrospect I know that I did little to help her in this entrepreneurial endeavor. It's one of those things you never forget about yourself and only hope that your mother forgives you for later on.

My main memories of the restaurant are the girls who worked for my mom. One girl was only a few years older than me and kind of liked me. I was so scared of girls at the time, like an idiot, that I avoided her flirting and hugs even though when she did them I always got excited, almost instantly.

The other girl was a young woman and she was, as we say now, a major babe. My primary recollection of her these many years hence, besides her lovely face, was her wonderful, high-sitting bosom. She had a thin, lovely body but, oh, my, as Jonathan Winters might say, upstairs was gangbusters! She was almost more than a thirteen year old boy could deal with.

After the restaurant closed down for lack of steady business we, my mother and I, went back to work at Jug's. If I haven't mentioned this before, every single member of my immediate family at one time or another worked at Jug's and even some of the spouses and significant others. It was a two-family operation much of the time. Jug's and ours. I got fifty cents an hour to wash dishes at Jug's. Big time. I worked four to midnight on Friday and Saturday nights and four to eight on Sundays. Twenty hours, ten dollars. It wasn't that bad for the time.

One day before the start of my sophomore year of high school I got into one of my uppity moods at Jug's and, against my mother's wishes and admonitions, quit, storming out of the place like I was some kind of untouchable potentate instead of the nerdy little punk kid that I was. Anyway, that finished my dishwashing days in Fayetteville. The next spring was when we moved to California, my mother going out in March of 1961, me following her at the end of the school year in late May.

So there it was. My working life to that point had been exclusively devoted to being a dishwasher and now it was late fall 1961 in Calipatria, California and I had to get a job again. What was there to do? Go straight to Williams's Café naturally. Luckily for me, the guy I was replacing at the café was a new football buddy from the high school, Sheldon, and he taught me the ropes at Williams's. They had a machine that did the dishwashing, which was a major advancement and time saver, and it turned out to be a decent enough job.

The main thing Sheldon taught me was how to manipulate the weekly food allowance. I've forgotten the exact amount of that allowance but Sheldon showed me that if you ate hamburgers and fries all week during your shift, by Saturday you would be able to treat yourself to a soft, juicy, tender filet mignon. I followed his advice to a T and it worked. Each Saturday afternoon I would take a break before the evening rush and have that filet mignon. Solid advice well taken.

Williams's Café turned out to be my last job as a dishwasher, save one horrible evening in Boulder, Colorado a little over ten years later, but that's another story for another time. The following spring, some of my buddies and I worked with the Mexican Braceros for a few weeks in the fields and then I landed a job helping the local electrician, for whom my mother had landed a job herself as sales clerk, bookkeeper, and what have you.

From that point on, like most young men, I worked at this job and that, this place and that, off and on, hither and yon, until I finally tried my best to become a permanent student. That, too, is a story for a later time.

What Passed for Fun
in the Desert

THIS IS WHAT passed for fun living out in the desert, at least as it involved motor vehicles, or something like them. Trying to reach 120 miles an hour in somebody's dad's car out on the straight stretch east of town. Tying bales of hay behind somebody's car and then standing on the bales so that you were surfing behind the car on some dirt road outside of town. This was a particularly intelligent thing to do. Even at ten or fifteen miles an hour, coming off that bale and crashing into a ditch can scrape you up at least a little bit.

Trust me on this one, too, please.

Here's the best one probably. If you let some air out of your car's tires and line the tires up with the tracks of a (preferably unused) train line, the car will cling to the tracks and you can simply press the gas and let go of the wheel. The car travels happily down the tracks like you worked for Burlington Northern and Santa Fe, really. The exciting part is crossing trestles several dozen feet above the ground, or water. That's a little hairy. But it's all lots of fun till you get to a crossroads. The track is as low as the road there and your vehicle will drop off the tracks unless you are careful. It's a good thing that's not true about halfway across one of those trestles, huh?

Trying to reach 120 miles an hour in somebody's dad's car out on the straight stretch east of town Don't try this at home, folks.

J. B. Hogan Collection

You've Got to Have a Better Reason to Go to Church Than That

I STOPPED GOING to church because one day while I was squawking away in choir—man I was a bad singer—I realized that the only reason I was in church was because my girlfriend was there. As I massacred another fine hymn, I couldn't stop looking at her. She seemed almost angelic in her long golden choir robe, and I couldn't think of anything else but her. She was beautiful. I loved her, and this church and religion stuff was no more than an excuse to be somewhere near her. That realization came to me in a moment of sharp clarity.

Even a heathen like myself can have some sort of morality or ethical standards, and so I understood then, on that day and at that moment, that I was a huge hypocrite for being in church. I no longer believed in that big god in the sky with the long, gray beard and the hard-ass attitude toward his flunky creations. What was that all about anyway? If he knew we were such screw ups, which he had to in his omniscience I reasoned, then what was the point?

To tell the truth, I never had the faith gene. At least that's what I tell people now. But I did grow up with some sort of belief in a Judeo-Christian god. Here are the exact reasons and moments along the way that rid me of my faith in any man-made traditional religion.

Trying to get myself saved at the Church of the Nazarene. When I was about ten or twelve or so, my mother, god rest her soul (how else can one say that?), started letting me make up my own mind whether I wanted to go to church or not. She had her own quiet, strong Methodist belief, but she never, ever, pushed it on her children or others. One Sunday I decided, why I don't know, to go to a relatively nearby Church of the Nazarene. During the service, the preacher called for people to come forward and get saved, to accept Jesus Christ as their personal savior.

Lifted by the spirit, I shuffled forward with several other people to accept our lord and savior into our hearts and lives. Man, I concentrated on this. I wanted to do this badly. The preacher was praying away, the other people were intently accepting Jesus, and I was working my fanny off to take in our Lord. At one point, the preacher even said, "Open up your hearts and let Jesus, your Lord and Savior, come in."

I redoubled my efforts. I swear I was even sweating, and I was waiting, waiting for Jesus to come, to come into my heart. I could hear some of the other people making sounds like they had succeeded. They were saved. But I wasn't. Nothing was happening. Jesus wasn't coming in. I imagined my heart opening wide, wider, and Jesus, looking like the kind young man on my Sunday School missal, light skin and wavy brown hair, coming to the door of my heart, ready to come in. But that was as far as I could get him. Only the image. No feeling. No glorious sensation of salvation, no Christ within.

Everybody else walked forward to the preacher, and he spoke words over all of them, welcoming them to the flock of the Lord. I went with them, knelt before the preacher, heard his words, but nothing had happened. Nobody came into my heart. All I had managed to conjure up was an image of Jesus, kind, wavy brown-haired Jesus, at the door of my poor feeble heart. I felt myself a complete and utter fraud. I knew I hadn't been saved. Nothing had happened at all. When I left church that morning, I was feeling down. I didn't go back to church much after that until high school.

A couple of summers later I had a kind of weird all-night marathon attempt to save me by some newly-converted kids at a boys' camp but that had faded as soon as the summer did. Then, when I was about fifteen, I lost my faith all in one fell swoop or swell foop as we like to say nowadays. At the time, it wasn't funny at all.

What happened was that I suddenly, from out of nowhere and without warning, lost all belief in God, religion, even spirituality. I mean it all went, all of it at once and it went fast. I associate it with this one night I was out late and the sky was clear and I was looking up at the stars and they were shining crisp and clear and distant in the heavens and the next thing I knew I was completely, totally overwhelmed by this powerful sense, an understanding, that all things must end, had to end, and ended forever. There's no heaven, no afterlife, no nothing. It would be all black and empty with consciousness gone.

How could that be? How could we lose our awareness, our sense of self and of all the things we've thought and done and dreamed about and hoped for. And yet that was all I saw then. There was no God. How could there be? Who would have made him? How could anything be eternal, infinite? None of that made any sense at all. Not anymore. And I felt trapped. Trapped by the illogical logic of existence itself.

Looking back, I've guessed it was my first clear realization of my own mortality hitting me like a brick between the eyes. But it was more than that, too. There was this idea that existence made no sense whatsoever. Why was there a universe, why was there a God, why was there anything at all? Why would that be? Why not nothing? Why did something have to be at all.

Whatever was going on in my mind, I felt a devastating wave of terror come over me. I was trapped, trapped in an existence that made no sense to me anymore, trapped by time and space, trapped by eternity, trapped by an illogical nothingness. It was not a pleasant experience, but finally, the terror I felt at feeling like I was trapped in the unfathomable and irrational web of existence lifted, lifted off my fifteen year old shoulders. I felt a wave of euphoria spread over me, a thankfulness that I did not have to stay constantly in such a horrifying state of mind.

Over the years, these moments of horrendous clarity would strike me at odd times, rendering me virtually catatonic until they would slowly pass, always being replaced by that soul-lifting feeling of euphoria that thankfully followed each episode. As I got older, the episodes were further and further apart and their intensity decreased in a similar fashion. Now I seldom have that feeling at all. Perhaps it's because I'm less afraid of dying now or at least think of it less often, even though it is far closer than it was when these attacks began.

Whatever the source or the meaning of these sensory assaults, the bottom line was that down inside, at the core of my being, whatever portion of faith I might have had remaining was gone. Excised as it were, cut from my soul with a metaphorical sharp knife.

Despite these intense episodes and my sense of no longer believing in anything, when I moved to California my first new friend turned out to be the son of the Baptist preacher in town, and I sort of fell back into attending church. Mostly as a social activity because it was a way to meet new kids my age and to interact positively with my new community. After about another year of going through the motions, I found myself in the position in which this narrative began, going to church to be near to and admire the physical beauty of my sweet girlfriend. Now that's not a bad reason, as reasons go, but my seventeen year old brain knew it was time to pack up the religion and stop being a big fat phony.

I have never set foot in a church since then for the purpose of worship. The next time I went inside a church was for services after JFK's assassination. When I went into the military the next year, I was so adamant about my lack of religious belief that I insisted they put NRP (No Religious Preference) on my dog tags. As this was one of the options, I got my wish. Jerry B. Hogan, O Pos, NRP. And so that was how my faith went away and how it still is today.

The Sleeping Hunter and a 184-Foot-Tall Christmas Tree (One Beautiful Christmas)

NOT EVERYTHING WE did in the Valley was about sewing wild oats or finding our way toward adulthood. There are some pleasant memories from that time as well. Once, for example, on a cool, breezy winter day, with the wind whipping the fine grains of sand off the desert topsoil and up against the side of my body and face, I decided to take my .22 bolt-action rifle and go shoot at ducks or whatever I could find either in the empty fields outside of town or in the irrigation canals that crisscross the Valley floor.

The sun was shining brightly and I put my head down into the wind and walked away from town until I was where I could shoot without bothering or endangering anyone else. For some reason, I wasn't interested in shooting anything that day and so I found an embankment by a canal that I could climb down on and get out of the wind. There was a big Tamarack tree by the canal and I lay beside it far enough down the dirt bank to use it as a windbreak. It was warm out of the wind and I lay there a few moments relaxing. I laid my rifle across my lap and soaked up the calm, tranquil world in my little island of windless warmth.

The next thing I knew I was waking up, not startled awake, but calmly waking up. I checked the level of the sun and guessed I had been asleep for close to two hours. I felt completely rested and total-

ly at peace with the world. For those two hours I had been outside
the world, no hassles, no teenage angst, no worries about the future,
completely at peace. It may have been the last time I slept so relaxed
in all my life.

I slowly stretched and stood up. There wasn't a soul around and
maybe there hadn't been anyone come by the entire time I slept. I
had my own private world for two hours of mind and body restoring
rest. Carrying my rifle in my right hand, I climbed up over the embankment and back onto the dirt road leading back to town and the
little apartment home that I shared with my mother. I took my time
going back. I felt good.

ONE OF THE things that distinguished our little town was that
its municipal flagpole was exactly the height that the town itself was
below sea level, 184 feet. It was a cool flagpole and for Christmas the
fire department strung wires of lights from the top of the pole to the
ground, making it the biggest Christmas tree I had ever seen. With
its alternating bulbs of reds, yellows, greens and so forth, also the
prettiest one, too.

I enjoyed this flagpole Christmas tree immensely, and you could
see it for several miles across the desert, especially when you were
coming into town from Brawley, the next town to our south. It made
you feel proud to be from this little bitty town that had such a big old
Christmas tree flagpole. It was cool.

One cool evening during my last Christmas in California, a rare
fog settled over the north end of the Valley covering our little town
and its flagpole tree in a thick, soupy white cloud. The fog by itself
was cool, but when it thinned a bit the lights on the flagpole were
visible in a beautiful, hazy multi-colored display.

I was so impressed with the fog and lights that I crawled out one of the back windows in our apartment and went onto the roof to get a better view. I stood at the westernmost edge of our apartment building and watched the fog cover and uncover the wondrous lights of the town's Christmas flagpole.

A powerful sense of the holiday season swept over me like the fog sweeping over the colored lights. My heart filled with joy and hope and optimism. It was the best Christmas I ever had because of that. And it was the last one in which I felt the purity and essence (that's a Doctor Strangelove reference for all you classic movie buffs) of the season. I have never been able to feel Christmas like that since and that is perhaps too bad, but I will always have this memory, and it will never leave me as long as I live.

Running from the CHP (They Didn't Call Them CHiPs Back Then)

IN JUNE OF 1963, I graduated from high school. High school graduation night, I've decided over the years, must be about the same for every kid, every year, and every place in the known universe. You celebrate too much, drink when you're not legal to, and say farewell to happy or unhappy high school days and to your high school friends and acquaintances. Mine, no doubt like thousands of others, was a bit on the wild side.

The strongest memory I have of the graduation part, or right after it to be specific, was being kissed, rather passionately, the minute we stormed out of the multi-purpose building where the graduation services had been held, by one of the prettiest girls in school, a lovely Filipino girl. She had been my friend for sure but had hitherto shown no such inclination toward physical contact with me. It was an amazing kiss and I was trying to figure out what to do about it when my buddies grabbed me and in two cars we stormed out of town. We headed south toward Brawley for presumably more kicks than our little town could provide and also with the prospect of picking up some booze and/or beer.

The two guys driving the packed cars, I can't remember who they were anymore, decided we should race to Brawley. So we were flying down the highway our headlights flashing across the huge cotton, lettuce, and tomato fields, side by side at what was probably between eighty and ninety miles an hour. Really fast was all I knew. As we rounded a turn not far out of our little town, the second car, the one I was in, suddenly dropped back behind the first. There was a lot of whooping and hollering and yelling at our driver for letting the other car get ahead.

About then, however, we saw why he had chosen to go back to legal, single file driving. A big, black Chrysler cruiser came roaring at us from the direction of Brawley. It was a CHP (California Highway Patrol, C-H-P, not CHiPs, like on that silly TV show) cruiser and he was hauling balls. I saw the CHP car blast past us and then hit his brakes, hard.

I'll never forget seeing those red brake lights out the back window of the car. I could see him fishtailing as he tried to control his vehicle, turn it around, and come after us. After all, we were seriously speeding and racing side by side. We didn't figure the CHP would be too pleased with any explanation we might have.

CALIPATRIA HIGH SCHOOL

1962·63

Wayne Dunaway, Principal

STUDENT SIGNATURE

GRADE

Student Identification Card

J. B. Hogan, high school ID, Calipatria, CA, 1963.
J. B. Hogan Collection

I yelled at the driver. "He's comin'. The CHP is turning around. He's coming after us."

There was another round of hollering in the car, but the driver did what any young guy would do in this situation. He completely put his foot into it. We were going to try and outrun the CHP. A sense of excitement and fear filled the car, and we yelled wildly as our car flew over the highway toward Brawley, shooting down into short valleys and over the New River (later designated the most polluted river in the U.S., though I believe it has been cleaned up since then) then up the next small hill and around curves our car was barely making.

It was madness and we were loving it. Somewhere in the blackness behind us was a CHP, his red lights flashing, big yellow head beams on bright, chasing a bunch of crazy kids. We had to run from that, there was no choice.

Suddenly our driver made a radical decision. He picked a road that ran off to our right, to the west, paralleling Brawley a few miles to its north, and he hit this road going at least fifty miles an hour. I swear. The car slid on the dirt beside the pavement, fish tailed, leaned hard to one side, but then settled down as the wheels caught the pavement. In a flash we were heading away from the main road at breakneck speed.

"Jesus Christ." Somebody yelled. "Great driving!"

"I'm goin' to turn out the lights." The driver surprised us again. "We'll run in the dark until we lose the CHP."

"Holy crap!" I exclaimed.

"Roll down the windows, everybody lean out and watch the side of the road. Keep me on the pavement. I ain't slowin' down."

Luckily, we had a bright moon and it was fairly easy to see the road, which was also luckily straight, and we kept the car between the sides of the road. It was amazing. I kept looking back toward the highway but there was no sign of the CHP. In a few minutes it was obvious he had missed us and continued on the main highway. We had lost him. It was a miracle.

A couple of minutes later we spotted a road to the left that took us on into Brawley and we took it, turning the lights back on and slowing down a lot. We drove casually into Brawley from the back-side of town and wound our way through to a drive-in restaurant about a block off Brawley's main east-west road.

Sure enough, while we were ordering hamburgers, fries, and cokes, we saw a big CHP car cruising through town heading west. It was almost certainly the guy we had ditched. We were excited to see him and excited about our close call and escape, but the mood in the car had settled down and we acted cool, like it was something we did all the time.

Looking back, there's all kinds of things you could say about that experience. How foolish it was, how lucky we were not to have had a car wreck, how absurd it was to try and outrun a highway patrolman, driving with the lights off and all. It's been a long time since that evening's wild ride, but I have to say that, bad idea or not, it certainly left me with a sharp memory of my graduation night.

Overall it was probably relatively tame compared to things that other, even wilder kids might do. The main thing about this type of memory is that you lived through it, made it to the other side so that you can tell people about it. It's the lucky ones who get to tell stories like this, and that's what we were that night, real lucky.

IVC Is the School
for Me

IVC WAS IMPERIAL Valley Junior College, a new JC built in the middle of scrub desert about five miles east of the city of Imperial. As I and my fellow seniors approached graduation, those of us who knew we would not be going on to a regular college, whether from financial or academic limitations, began to seriously entertain the idea of attending IVC.

In those days, the state of California guaranteed two years of basically free higher education after high school. All you had to pay for was a student body card. It was an extraordinary opportunity. IVC was one of those places you could go to virtually for free and so we began to sing a little song around school late in my senior year.

The song, extremely simple, even by our standards, was "IVC is the school for me." We would sing this one-line song over and over to each other in the school hallways, on the sports practice fields, and when we gathered together in a vain attempt to alleviate our teenage boredom. It was clearly, even to us, an ironic reminder, with no offense to IVC, of our limited possibilities in the academic world.

I began attending classes at IVC in late August 1963. I think, for reasons beyond me now, I began as a Political Science major. It didn't matter much what I was supposed to be concentrating on because with all the free time we had between classes (so different than high school days I quickly learned) I was shortly doing little or no academic work whatsoever.

I made sure I signed up to try out the following spring for the baseball team and I kept my fall grades above the required 2.0 GPA in order to be eligible to play but that was it. I was soon hanging with some of my old high school buds and some new ones I made on campus and what we did mostly was nothing.

We started skipping classes to play ping pong, there was a competitive circle of players each of us with our own personal paddle, or the card game Whist, which took up hour upon idle hour. Even worse, we started leaving campus after somebody discovered a pool hall at a bowling alley out on the main highway just outside Imperial.

Eight Ball was our usual game until someone got us onto the snooker tables and even a billiard one. Snooker helps your eight ball game because the balls and the holes on the table are so tiny compared to the ones in eight ball. And billiards is excellent for learning how to use rails and so forth. All of these are required skills if you plan to make a living as a pool hustler. As for their impact on your average college student's academics, well, does the phrase "wasted youth" ring a bell?

The fall of 1963, in retrospect, was a watershed time in American history. At the time, of course, we didn't know that, but we would soon. I remember Friday, November 22 as if it happened yesterday. I had finished my Humanities class, which I enjoyed and did all right in, and was heading over to the union to get a hamburger and probably play cards or pool. One of my Calipat buddies caught me on the way. He had just got to school and was coming on campus from a nearby parking lot.

"Hey." He hollered at me, excited like. "They something something someone."

"What?" I couldn't understand him.

"They shot the president." He repeated what he had apparently called out before.

"Sure." I figured he was pulling some kind of prank.

"No, honest, somebody shot JFK."

We took off for the union, then, joining groups of other students who kept filing in. Somebody set out a radio in the small courtyard area where we usually played cards or ping pong and everyone gathered around. Finally, the newsman announced the president's death. Some of the girls cried, some boys acted like it didn't bother them, most of us were too stunned to do or say anything.

My mother and I didn't have a TV then and on the weekend I worked out in the country cleaning up around a farm. The farm belonged to a guy who worked for my cousin Lloyd at the Imperial Hardware Store in town and his mom. It was a few miles west of town so I didn't get much direct information about the aftermath of the shooting.

I heard about Ruby shooting Oswald from other friends over the weekend and I remember going through the work of that weekend in a sort of daze. I also remember I had trouble believing that this sort of thing could happen in modern America. I thought the wild west days were over, but Dallas sure made it seem like we were back in them all right. It had been a regular shoot 'em up. America in its less than finest hour.

There were a lot more of these incidents to come, but we didn't know it then. It was probably a good thing we didn't. All the assassinations during that time sure didn't square with what most of us had been taught about our American way of life, and they still don't. They never have and they never will. Ever.

If They'd Only Had
an Outfield Fence

WHEN THE SPRING of 1964 finally rolled around, most of the pain of JFK's shooting had been sublimated, and I, for one, was happy it was baseball season. I went out for IVC's baseball team and made it. Considering I was five feet seven inches tall and weighed one hundred and twenty-five pounds soaking wet, I did all right.

We practiced and played in El Centro, using their cool, old minor league baseball stadium on the east side of downtown as our home park. Part of the bleachers were covered, the outfield was well kept and beautifully green, and there was even a grass infield. That was big time. We practiced at eight a.m., and luckily I found a ride with a guy from Calipat who worked in El Centro, and he dropped me off at the field each day.

This fine young man, whose first name was Dwayne or Duane, ended up being an early draftee into the Viet Nam War and was one of its earliest casualties. With my cousin Roy "Teenie" Allen and the other boys from Calipat who were killed in Korea and those who were shot up badly in both wars, it seemed that our little desert hometown paid a steep price for its service to the country.

As for baseball—when you made the IVC team, each player got to go to a sporting goods store in El Centro near the ballpark and

Arabs Take Over SCC League Race

IMPERIAL — The conference-leading Imperial Valley college baseball squad steps out of the league today for a non-loop doubleheader with the College of the Desert Roadrunners.

The Arabs three and one in conference play and riding the crest of a four game winning streak, will be out to knock off the Roadrunners while getting in form for a league tilt with the powerful Oceanside-Carlsbad Spartans April 4.

The Arabs split a pair with Palomar March 14 to open the four game win streak, trounced Palo Verde 14-11 Friday and captured both ends of a doubleheader at Santa Barbara Saturday, holding the Vaqueros to a single run in each and winning easily, 11-1 and 8-1.

Arab hurler Raul Alvorado started at Palo Verde and shut the Pirates out for two innings before being knocked off of the mound as the Verdians started connecting for six runs in the third inning. John Ramey took over the reins and held off the Pirates until the fifth when Hice Stiles took the mound. Mal Wagstaff caught for the Arabs.

Bill Winfree slapped a shot over the right center field fence for the first Arab home run of the season and batted in four runs while going three for five at the plate.

Eddie Hong and Jerry Hogan each smashed out three hit sfor the IVC nine and Frank Arviso and King Kimball each got two safetys.

The Arabs picked up 14 runs on 17 hits and two errors. Palo Verde had 11 runs on eight hits and four errors.

In the first stanza of the Arab-Santa-Barbara doubleheader, IVC bombed Vaquero star pitcher Jim Peirson for three runs in the first inning and four in the fourth before he retired in favor of relief hurler Tracy. Eight Arabs beat out hits, six of them blasting two safetys and Hank White picking up three singles.

Hurler Tony Macias beat out a triple and a single and Dick a triple and a single and Dick Reital fired a shot off the right center field wall for a three-bagger.

Macias finished the game with 11 strikeouts without walking a single Vaquero before being relieved.

The IVC nine had 11 runs on 15 hits and one error while Santa Barbara finished with one run on four hits and three errors.

The Arabs capped the day with the 8-1 win over the hosts behind the pitching of John Bishop and relief Larry Mostrong who played relief roles in both games.

Reital paced the Arab batsmen with a triple, single and a walk while Winfree, Hong, White and Bishop each pounded out two singles.

Kimball rapped out a double and Mostrong and Wagstaff each had a single to round out the Arab batting force.

The Arabs finished with eight runs on 14 hits and one error and the Vaqueros had one run on two hits and one error.

Starting pitchers for today's contest are Sti'les and Wagstaff. Play starts at 1 p.m. at COD.

didn't look like a fight from this side of the Rockies. A Gilbert and Sullivan musical maybe, but not a fight.

Sonny didn't answer the bell and Clay answered it before it rang — a new champion had arrived (the crown shifted heads). If anyone entertained thoughts about the weight of the crown and the splendor of the throne humbling yon Cas-

Wildcat Ten: Lose To Kof

BRAWLEY — Brawley High School's varsity tennis team dropped a 4-3 decision at Kofa High School Saturday and the Wildcat's girl netters were shut out by Kofa 7-0.'

The varsity boys were able to capture the middle two matches but dropped three im-McKissick of Brawley defeated Ed Tallbert, 6-4,9-7, for a singles victory and Robert Alcala nudged Herb Huttner, 3-6, 6-2, 6-1, for the other win.

Alcala teamed with Wally Ulloa to defeat Tallberg and Huttner, 4-6, 6-2, 6-2, to gain a split for the Wildcats in doubles play. In other singles matches, Dave Anderson of Kofa defeated Joe Cortez, 6-2, 6-1; Tom Gardner of Kofa defeated Ulloa, 6-4, 4-6, 6-0; and Kofa's Gordon Helm topped Joe Alderete, 6-2, 6-2, 6-1. Anderson and Gardner grabbed a 6-2, 1-6, 6-1, doubles victory over Cortez and McKissick.

Brawley's girls found the gals

IVC Owns Top Spot In Loop

South - Central Conference standings:

Team	W	L	Pct.
Imperial Valley College	3	1	.750
Oceanside-Carlsbad	3	3	.500
Palomar	3	3	.500
Santa Barbara	2	2	.500
Antelope Valley	1	3	.250

Imperial Valley (CA) College, Baseball Clipping, 1964.
J. B. Hogan Collection

select two bats apiece. Man, that was something. Two bats and not have to pay a dime. I was happier than a clam. I used to love the old Nelson Fox bottle bats, but they had already fallen out of favor by then and I had to settle for two bats with the thickest handles I could find. They still weren't even close to the fatness of the Nellie Fox, my all-time favorite bat.

I got off to a good start once the season began. The guy who beat me out for second base on the team missed some early games, and I got to start instead. I got two hits and a couple of walks and scored some runs in an opening non-conference doubleheader and then a few games later went three for four in a game up at Coachella Valley JC.

But something happened then. I still don't know what it was, but I got in the coach's doghouse and he only started me one other time, when Coachella Valley came to play us in El Centro (I went "ofer" in that game, no hits) and all I got to do the rest of the year was pinch hit.

The team was terrific, however, and we won the South Central Conference easily, eventually losing in the first round of the state Southern California JC tournament. The last game of the regular season, before the state tourney, we played at Palm Desert JC. It was Palm Desert's first year fielding a team and we played them a non-conference doubleheader. The coach held me out until our last time at bat in the second game. We were down by one run, with one out and a runner at first base. Here's how the at bat went down.

The coach hollered at me to get a bat. I had been sitting on the bench for hours and it had been colder than expected. My hands were chilled and I was sort of stiff. Regardless, I hustled off the bench and grabbed one of my bats. I went through my usual pre-at bat routine. I would swing two or three bats together a few times, toss all but mine behind me toward the dugout and then stroll up to the plate.

At the plate I had a brief ritual. I would take a few practice swings and stretch a little bit. Before stepping into the batter's box, I would take a couple of regular swings then bend down and scoop a small amount of dirt into the palms of my hands, spit into that and rub my hands together to give me a solid grip on the bat. Now I was ready to hit.

The pitcher on the other team was not a super hard thrower and his best pitch was a big, roundhouse curveball. As a left-handed batter I could see that curve coming a mile away. I managed to work him to a full count, I had a good eye in those days, and right before he delivered the payoff pitch I heard his coach or someone yell out "strike him out." For some reason I was sure that was a signal for the curveball. Whether it was or not, I guessed right. It was a curveball.

I can still see that baby coming at me. Big, fat, round. Hooking right into my wheelhouse. Right into my swing. I hit that ball as hard as I've ever hit any ball in my life, little guy or not. It fairly sailed. Straight toward the gap in right-center field. I had hit it full bore. It looked like it would go forever. Turned out there was one minor problem. Palm Desert was such a new school, their field didn't have a fence. That meant the right fielder could keep running and running and running.

And that's what happened. He ran and ran until the ball began to die and he made a fine, long, running catch. With a regulation distance fence, the ball might have hit it, bounced into it, or even cleared it. As it was, my mighty hit was caught. It was just a long, loud out.

Worse yet, our runner, who had taken off from first base believing the ball was either gone or going to land in the alley and roll forever, was way around second base when the catch was made. He was so far from first that the relays easily doubled him up before he could get back to first. Instead of a game-tying or winning hit, I had delivered a game-ending double play with a long fly ball out.

That turned out to be my last official at bat in my last officially competitive baseball game. When I think about it, though, that wasn't such a bad way to end my baseball career. I had guessed the pitch right, I had hit it as squarely and as hard as I could. I would have liked a different outcome but, hey, at least I tagged the ball really good. That's a heck of a lot better than having a final strikeout to remember or, worse yet, no memory of having played ball at all. Never having played baseball at all? Now that would be a truly terrible memory to have.

Into the Old
Wild Blue Yonder

I BELIEVE IT was March of 1964 when the Beatles first appeared on Ed Sullivan. I remember the buzz about them had started in the fall of 1963, and their records were starting to get some serious rotation time on the rock stations. I was certain, however, that it was all hype. And I wasn't going to fall for it.

Skeptically, I went over to one of my buddy's houses where they had a tube and we settled down to check out these upstart, overblown British punks. Oh, yeah, yeah, yeah. What was a Beatle anyway, a lame version of a Cricket, right? Think Buddy Holly and the Crickets. Anyway, I was so ready to write these guys off. They were too much, too big for their britches. I was having none of that. No, sir, not a bit of it... uh, that is, until the first note of the first song they sang. Oops, guess which eighteen year old was completely wrong.

I loved the Beatles instantly and was bowled over by the British Invasion in general. The music came alive in a way that it had not since the days when Elvis and the rockers and the R&B people first showed up to knock the old style pop music off the top of the charts. It was exciting, and I fully embraced it.

What I didn't embrace was the idea of going on to school or of working the rest of my life in some physical labor job there in the Imperial Valley. Not that there is anything wrong with that, I just knew it wasn't for me, that's all.

So in mid-July 1964, after spending the first part of the summer caretaking a fruit garden and pulling out wooden cherry tomato stakes in the 115 plus degree heat on a small farm outside Niland in the absolute middle of nowhere desert, I decided to join the U.S. Air Force. I thought I would at least get training in some useful field that I could find work in when I got out. Both my brothers had done that and it seemed to have worked for them, why not me.

July 13, 1964, the day I was inducted into the Air Force. The day before I had taken a bus from Brawley where my mother and a friend of mine dropped me off at the station for the trip up to Los Angeles and the Induction Center. Me and my buddy shook hands and

Airman Jerry B. Hogan, son of Mrs. Martha P. Hogan of Calipatria, Calif., has completed the first phase of his Air Force basic military training at Lackland AFB, Texas.

Airman Hogan has been selected for technical training as a communications specialist at an Air Training Command (ATC) school at Keesler AFB, Miss. His new unit is part of the vast ATC system which trains airmen and officer in the diverse skills required by the nation's aerospace force. Airman Hogan, a graduate of Calipatria High School, attended Imperial Valley Junior College.

USAF Basic Training, Lackland AFB, San Antonio, TX, in Calipatria Herald, *1964. J. B. Hogan Collection*

pretended it was no big deal my leaving, but when it came time to say goodbye to my mom it wasn't so easy. She cried a little bit and I kind of choked up. I remember seeing them out the darkly-tinted window of the bus as it pulled away.

The bus route went right back through my little town of Calipat and I peered out the window to see if I could spot any of my friends but no one was out on the hot streets and we were shortly barreling up the road to Indio at the far north end of the Salton Sea.

Millions of young guys have been inducted into the various branches of the service and I'm sure it's the same for all of them. Feeling uncomfortable, hanging with new guys you don't know (I met two boys from Terre Haute, Indiana who were the most racist people I had ever met up to that point, darn near still the worst I ever met), peeing in bottles, having doctors probe and pry you, getting shots, and then shipping out to your basic training base.

Lackland Air Force Base in San Antonio, Texas is the Air Force's big basic training base (except for a stretch in the '60s when they opened up another one in Amarillo I believe it was to accommodate the huge excess of enlistees trying to avoid combat in Viet Nam), and I went there like zillions of young men before me.

The flight out of L.A. was the first time I had ever been on an airplane. Naturally it was delayed by an electrical problem, but we finally took off, the revving up of the engines before we took off was particularly exciting to me, and landed in San Antonio sometime in the middle of the night. You always arrive at your first bases in the middle of the night, especially basic and training bases. They want you off guard, out of kilter, not ready for whatever surprises they have in store for you.

The main thing I remember about my first night of basic is that one kid from our group, we were all California inductees, went AWOL sometime before we were rousted out the next morning for our first day of training. Even now that seems an amazing thing to me. The guy couldn't even make it through one night? Unbelievable. Word was it was because he was missing his girlfriend. I believe he was allowed to get out of the service without a problem. I'm sure that was the right decision. Man, if you can't even do the first night, you definitely do not belong in.

Basic Training—Oh, Boy, Only 3 Years, 10 months, and 3 weeks Left to Go

THE MOST HUMILATING thing about Air Force basic training back in the day was that for the first four or five days, even up to a week, they make you march around in your civvies. Well, this gives every sack of you know what who has been in basic for a few days longer than you the chance to make fun of you in your civilian clothes, to pull rank on you. You feel like a major dork until you get your fatigues and brogans and get to pretend that you're an experienced military guy yourself and then you can make fun of the new guys in their civvies. See how that works?

Air Force basic was, of course, vastly easier than the Army and Marines. All we did was march a lot, do KP and other menial jobs, exercise on the PT fields, and do a simple obstacle course. I was so geared up to do well on the obstacle course, which I ran on my birthday by the way, that when I came to this log jump where you land on one log and then spring up to the next, I darned near gave myself a deep thigh bruise by turning myself into a projectile and almost flying over the entire upper log. I recovered fine, thank you, but I was close to missing that second log and doing an embarrassing header into the ground. I'm sure I looked silly if anybody noticed me.

These are some of the memories of basic that have stuck with me over the years. Rappelling off a hill during the obstacle course, normally I'm afraid of any heights but for some reason I liked that rappelling. Getting food poisoning the night before we had our first KP assignment (I was weak as a tiny little kitten when we marched off to the chow hall at three a.m. the next morning, but I somehow recovered quickly and made it through the day okay). Watching the Lackland Warhawks, the base baseball team, playing on their field right behind my barracks, we sometimes stayed up after lights out to see what we could of the games. And listening to the "House of the Rising Sun" by the Animals on the radio anytime we had a moment to turn one on, the song was a massive hit that summer.

I also remember the TIs (Technical Instructors the Air Force called them then) getting up in people's faces and saying stuff that is funny to me now ("What you lookin' for, boy," one TI used to yell at this poor kid who couldn't salute worth a

USAF Extended Basic Training, Keesler AFB, Biloxi, MS, Fall 1964.
J. B. Hogan Collection

darn, "Indians?"). I remember an E-2 (Airman Third Class then) getting in my face for no reason one time. That still isn't funny to me. I'd like to go back to that moment for sure and straighten him out. Smoke breaks where I would drink water and bloat up until I finally started smoking, too. It only took me sixteen years to quit smoking, that's all.

Sometime during the fifth week of basic training, which ended up being all the basic I did at Lackland, the idea that I might have made a big mistake in joining the service began to creep into my consciousness. I didn't like the yelling, the bossing around, the fact that people seemed to be telling you stupid crap and expecting you to believe and follow it unthinkingly.

Oh, yeah, I came in with an attitude all right, no doubt about that. But I was quickly convinced that most of these guys were dumb, me being so smart and all, and I didn't like their telling me what to do all the time. Oops, problem with authority. Didn't know I had that. But I found out quickly enough. I did a fast calculation of how long I had left to go. Three years, ten months, and three weeks. Oh, crap. I had screwed up this time.

So, there I was, a dummy in a dumb situation. What was there to do about it? Nothing. You had to get on with it, that was all. At the end of the first half of basic, the five week intro course, I was shipped out to Keesler Air Force Base in Biloxi, Mississippi. At least it was a change of scenery, maybe things would go better there.

Tech School—This Is No Time to Get Into Folk Music

THINGS DID GO better at Keesler, for a couple of months anyway. While I was waiting for technical school to begin I did three weeks of extra detail. One week of grounds keeping, one week of KP, and then back to grounds keeping. The grounds keeping, mowing lawns, clipping grass off curbs and such, was hot and miserable but the KP was great. I got the job of milkman, an easy job. All you did all day was replace the canisters of milk in these canister holding things. You tote out a fresh, full canister, remove the empty, put the new one in place, cut off the end of the rubber nozzle to allow the milk to be dispensed, wipe up any small spills, then haul the empty away and that was that. Great job.

How did I get to Keesler you might ask? Well, in basic training they have you take a bunch of tests and then they interview you and ask you what career path you'd like to pursue during your Air Force career. Being the know it all that I was, when the sergeant interviewing me asked if I was interested in Intelligence I thought that meant something to do with brain power and so I said, "Yes, sir, I like the sound of that."

Of course I liked the sound of it. I was so stupid I thought it had the same meaning as the civilian word intelligence. Silly me. Plus, the other two options the guy wrote down for me, something or other

J. B. Hogan in civilian clothes, Morse Intercept Operator Training, Keesler AFB,
Biloxi, MS, early Fall 1964.
J. B. Hogan Collection

and Supply, both sounded bad. I realized later that I had done okay on the Morse Code part of my basic training tests and the USAFSS (U.S. Air Force Security Service) needed operators; ergo, I was to be shipped to Keesler AFB to be trained as a Morse intercept operator. At the time, of course, I thought I was going off to do something brilliant and brain challenging.

AND THEN, THERE I was. Biloxi, Mississippi. Keesler Air Force Base. Morse Intercept Operator school. I was on my way now. They were training me to copy the Morse code. And Morse school was highly stimulating and competitive. I liked learning to copy code, oddly enough I liked marching, too, and I liked my new buddies, at least most of them. But, unfortunately, that was about all I did like.

I began to exhibit my rebellious nature at Keesler, not cleaning and shining my brogans good enough, getting a little bit huffy with an occasional "superior" (just another airman but with more status than I had), and generally pushing back a little at the mindless, in my opinion, authoritarian attitude that prevailed in this environment.

For reasons I still don't quite understand, I was okay with marching to school. I kind of enjoyed it. And I did like trying to be the first guy to a new level of the code (we learned in increments, five words per minute, eight words per minute, along those lines, up to eighteen point five, which was what you had to pass to move on to a permanent assignment).

I remember two marching incidents that stand out after all these years. One morning when we were marching to school, Vonda Kay Van Dyke, the reigning Miss America, was on the review stand. Nobody minded doing the "eyes right" order that day, that was for sure.

And one time, after school, as my unit marched back into our barracks area, the guys in our unit who were taking classes in the morning, called A Shift (at this time I had finished my extended basic training and was in the second half of my Morse class, which was in the afternoon, or B Shift) were yelling at us from the windows of the barracks.

Our White Rope, the main student leader who wore a white rope on the shoulder of his uniform, let it all hang out for a change that day and gave us the "fingers right" command. That was great. As we marched up, at his command we all did an eyes right and then raised our right arms with middle finger extended. Our A Shift brethren hooted and hollered again, but we won that one. For a change, we got a good laugh out of being at Keesler.

Keesler wasn't all that bad. Not really. I'm not sure I can say the same about Biloxi. Not without lying anyway. Biloxi completely threw me. It was a decent-looking little town, next to the Gulf and all. It had Jefferson Davis' home there, a big shrimping industry, moderate weather (though it felt too hot in summer and too cool in winter), and lots of places for a GI to eat and drink. Howsomever, the town had its drawbacks.

For example, as I remember it, the entire state of Mississippi was dry at the time I was at Keesler but there were bars all over Biloxi. Downtown (with cops outside, no less), on the back side of the base, out by the beach. And you could go into any one of them and drink beer and mixed drinks and nobody thought a thing about it and they didn't ask you your age. I'm thinking the local entrepreneurs didn't want to lose all that military money that was waiting on base ready to be spent in Biloxi.

Gambling was also illegal, but there were little gambling shacks around here and there, one right down by the coastal highway. And you could go in and place a bet on a race in Santa Anita back out in California if you were so inclined. A number of the bars that catered to GIs also had slot machines and the like. It was wide open, the drinking and the gambling that is.

There was even a dirty movie house not far from downtown.

Crappy joint. You know, the sort of place where you half expected guys to show up in rain coats and sit with bags of popcorn over their crotches. I mean it was trashy. One visit was all I needed.

If you kept going on down to the beach, kind of on the southeast edge of Biloxi, as I recall, there was a big old two-story southern home used as the USO. Now, USOs do a lot of good for servicemen and I'm not putting them down whatsoever, but they're not where rowdy GIs typically hang out. In fact, this one in Biloxi was the last one that I ever went to (the first had been on a weekend pass to San Antonio while in basic training). One of the reasons was that at this one in Biloxi I saw one of the saddest and most troubling things I ever saw during my service days.

The Biloxi USO was set up so that lonely airmen could meet and possibly hook up with, no doubt, even lonelier local girls. Since the ratio of guys to girls was probably at least ten to one in the USO, I figured I had zero chance and hung back from the scene, snacking on cookies and sipping punch or lemonade (see why my kind of GI didn't hang out there much?).

Anyway, I'd been in there about ten minutes or so when I saw her. An unfortunate girl. Looking back, I guess the poor thing must've been a Thalidomide baby, it's all I could figure. She was attractive, young and dark-haired, vivacious, a remarkable trait considering she did not have any arms. That's not quite right. What she had were little partial arms barely coming out of her shoulders and little flipper hands. It was freaky to a young guy with not much worldly experience.

Also in retrospect, I have to admire this girl for her courage. At the time, however, seeing her there, mingling with the horny GIs from Keesler, made me feel weird. It seemed like giving herself to the GIs was maybe all this girl had and that made me uncomfortable, for myself, and sad, for her. My nineteen year old response was to eat that cookie and drink that lemonade as fast as I could and get the heck out of that USO. Which I did, and never went back. To that one or any other.

One last comment about Biloxi. For a town heavily dependent on the air base for its livelihood, Biloxi could be hostile to young airmen. One time a buddy and I stopped at a restaurant, I think it might have been the day we hustled out of that USO, on our way back uptown. When we walked into this restaurant, everybody in there stopped what they were doing and stared at us. The joint got completely quiet. You could hear a pin drop, as the old cliché goes, and it was true.

We sort of sized the place up, did a little bit of the old soft shoe back out the door. We headed uptown where you could walk past the policeman who was not enforcing the statewide drinking ban and into a bar full of other GIs and have a beer or two and some sort of snack like a pickled egg or spicy sausage or something. Then we headed back to base, wiser but not particularly happier for having gained that little piece of wisdom.

Back on base, me and some of my buddies tended to congregate in one guy's room, Joe was his name and he was from Philadelphia, a good guy and a little bit older than the rest of us as I recall. There was a group of about five or six of us and we were, god knows why, all getting into folk music at about the same time. I had first heard about Bob Dylan when I was playing on the IVC baseball team back in California and so I bought a couple of his early albums to check them out. I thought he was funny and profound and that talking blues stuff was way cool.

Besides my Dylan albums, we began listening to Joan Baez. We were all in love with her. She was not only pretty but had the most beautiful voice any of us had ever heard in our lives. Then I tacked on a Pete Seeger album, "I Can See a New Day," and we were off and running. We would drink beer, smoke cigarettes, listen to our folkie heroes, and discuss all the major issues that all young guys do when they are becoming grown, thinking men.

I, myself, even took on an intellectual pose. I would sit in my barracks room smoking a pipe and reading *War and Peace*. Oh, yeah, I was a major intellectual, trapped in the Air Force, trapped in this world that was becoming more uncool by the minute.

This was the fall of 1964, I would remind you. I was nineteen years old and didn't know my you-know-what from a hole in the ground. I thought I was becoming cool and hip. The Air Force, which owned me for the next three and a half years plus, was exactly the opposite in my not so humble opinion. You can't see any problems coming, can you? I didn't either. But they were on their way, courtesy of yours truly.

Spy World

THERE'S NO REAL way to describe what we did in Japan. At least not without incurring the wrath of the straight arrows who served there. And maybe even some die hard cold war NSA types who had, through the command structure of the USAFSS, put the fear of god into us airmen about the lifelong importance of the Top Secret information we were privy to.

The two-year assignment in Misawa meant you were there for 730 days, give or take a couple. I and several of my buddies were drunk for probably about half of those days, give or take a few dozen. Anyway, my job and lots of other guys as well, was listening to the Morse code.

We were supposedly selected for the stability of our personalities, that's a funny one, and because we all passed a relatively thorough background check by the old OSI in order to get the Top Secret clearance that we needed to be in the USAFSS. The OSI did interview family and friends of mine back in California because my friends and family wrote me about it while I was in Japan.

Anyway, at Misawa we worked rotating shifts with small breaks (about a day off) in between three- or four-day shifts (the shifts were days, swings, and mids). After each full cycle, we had a big break (three days off at first, then four after we went from a 3-1, 3-1, 3-3 shift cycle to 4-1, 4-1, 4-4).

J. B. Hogan, second row in jacket and baseball cap, with Flight One (Trick 1) buddies, 6921 Security Wing, Misawa AB, Japan, 1966.
J. B. Hogan Collection

This is all I'm going to say about what we did for now. As Morse intercept operators we listened to signals emanating from places that might have been well beyond the borders of northern Japan. Since this was in the absolute heart of the Cold War, you might look at a map of that region of the world and draw your own conclusions as to who we were listening to. See how well they taught me about security?

What we did, way too much and way too often, was drink and raise hell in AP Alley, a small area beyond the base's main gate that was thickly populated with bars, prostitutes, pimps, bartenders, and young GIs. It was a wild scene in the alley basically all the time.

Since there were four flights to accommodate the rotating shifts we did, one flight was always on big break while the others were working through their cycle of shifts. There was another, much smaller area of bars farther up in town called Sake Alley but it was usually only visited by the more adventurous roaming airmen. Of course I was one of those because that's how I knew about Sake Alley, duh.

When I first got to Misawa, I was still heavy into that folk thing that me and my tech school buddies back in Biloxi had gotten into. I was sort of a budding, latter day beatnik or something, at least that's what I thought—I think. The guy who trained me in Misawa, Daz, whom I consider a good friend to this day, had to put up with my "this ain't my thing" kind of attitude when I started work. And my first roommate, Vic, had to put up with my Dylan, Baez, Seeger, and various other folkie albums. He was a great guy but he made fun of my music unmercifully. Finally, I would only play my records when Vic was out.

I said I wasn't going to say any more about my work, but I lied. One other thing. Where we worked at the compound, which we called the gig, I often sat right in front of a big plexiglass board upon which other airmen charted the information I and other operators received. We were looking at the board from behind but you could see through it and so we knew what was going on not only from our code taking but from the markings on that board.

What was on the board, you might ask? Well, without giving out national security secrets that were no doubt declassified thirty years ago, suffice it to say that it involved air activity in the region. Remember when that KAL airliner was shot down a number of years ago? Well, if Misawa was still up and running like it was when I was there, that KAL liner would have been closely monitored and tracked on that big board—in real time. Get my drift? Thank you very much.

Storch, Hogan, and Culey in Sendai

NOT COUNTING A brief trip to the little coastal town of Hachinohe, near Misawa, when I first got to Japan, I only made three trips away from the local area in my entire two years there. The rest of the time was taken up in drunken frenzies down in AP and Sake Alleys as described before.

Me and several of my close buds spent one big break at Lake Towada, a mountainous resort area less visited by American service people. The lake was huge and cold and deep. The little town was pleasant and the people likewise, although they tended to gawk at us a little because, apparently, Americans didn't come there so much. We had a fun time because, for about the only time in my Japan tour, we interacted with normal, everyday Japanese people. It was great.

Another big trip was in late fall 1966 when our entire flight, at least most of us, took a train up to the port city of Aomori and hopped a good-sized ferry across a sea channel to the big port city of Hakodate on the northernmost island of Hokkaido. You might have heard of Sapporo, the famous city on Hokkaido where they have that cool festival each winter with all the incredible ice carvings. Sapporo is also the brand of beer that we GIs swilled by the gallons while we were over there.

Well, a couple of months earlier, in late September or early Octo-

ber I believe, a couple of my buddies and I heard that the Los Angeles
Dodgers were doing a Japanese tour after they had won the world
series. The Dodgers were going around the country playing Japanese
professional baseball teams, sometimes all-star squads. One of those
games was going to be in Sendai, about halfway between Tokyo and
Misawa, and it was going to be during one of our big breaks.

My friends Jerry and Curley and I took the train down to Sendai
and stayed in the Sendai Hotel. After signing in, Curley and I used
our own names but Jerry had, and has, a rowdy, playful streak and
signed himself in as Larry Storch, one of the stars of F Troop. After
settling in at the hotel, we went out and walked around the town,
gawking like tourists. At one point we were happily accosted by a
pack of cute little Japanese schoolchildren who wanted to practice
their English on these rare American visitors.

Later on, we found our way to a big department store where we
bought presents for our moms and family back home. I bought my
mom a large and stylish purple ashtray with matching cigarette light-
er. She still had both of them, kept with her all those years later, when
she passed away in 1999. It wasn't much of a gift I'll grant you that,
but I'm sure glad I got it for her. She always made you feel like the
crappiest little present you gave her was special, important. Some
moms are about as good as it gets. My mom was one of those.

Of course, after our busy day in Sendai, we fell back on what we
knew best. We went out and drank ourselves silly in some local bars.
That practically goes without saying doesn't it. Anyway, the game the
next day was absolutely great.

It was cool to see the Dodgers up close and personal in the little
baseball stadium in Sendai. They were staying at the Sendai Hotel
where we were, too, and we saw a couple of them on the elevator one
time. As I recall, L. A. won the game over the Tokyo (later Yomiuri)
Giants but that is a secondary memory for me.

What stands out on this trip was that we got to see two of the greatest Japanese baseball players of all time in that one game. Shigeo Nagashima was the third baseman for the Giants and the first baseman was, drum roll for baseball fans here, none other than Sadaharu Oh, the greatest homerun hitter of all time in all of the world.

Not only was it a real kick to see Oh, but the big man did us all a big memory favor, he blasted a homerun into the right field bleachers. Yes, sir, he came through big time, and against the world champs. That made the three of us part of a small group of foreigners who ever saw Sadaharu Oh play in his prime (or close to it) and of an even smaller group who saw him hit a homerun in person. Cool. Big time cool.

So, when all the fun was over and it was time to head back to Misawa, we went to the front desk of the hotel to check out. As we pooled our yen to pay up, the clerk handed us our bill. We checked it over and then all three of us broke up laughing.

The typed up bill listed our names as Storch, Hogan, and Culey. I know maybe you would've had to be there to get the full affect this had on us, but with Jerry using Larry Storch's name and Curley's name coming out last and sounding like Coolie and all. Well, it was more than we could stand. We laughed until the clerk must've figured we were completely nuts. Of course, he wasn't too far off.

Welcome to North Carolina, Now Go Home

SEYMOUR-JOHNSON AIR Force Base was located kind of on the southeast edge of Goldsboro, North Carolina. Once again I found myself in one of those little redneck southern military towns where the locals hated you but liked to take whatever money you had to spend. It's not that these towns were so bad, but there's always a tension between locals and the military people who, to the annoyance of both parties, have a symbiotic economic relationship to one another.

It turned out that Seymour-Johnson was close to the base I had requested when I cross-trained out of the USAFSS, a mutually agreed upon separation, I might add. Like basic training when I had a chance to list my top three job areas, when I left Misawa I was asked to list my top three choices for new bases back in the states. I can't remember my other two choices anymore, but number one was Myrtle Beach AFB, South Carolina.

Oh, yeah, can you imagine a better place to be assigned? It was a fighter wing and situated not more than a few miles from the beach. Myrtle Beach is a fine tourist town with beautiful beaches and all, and it seemed like a GI's paradise, what with the number of young women who undoubtedly were in town most of the months of the year.

So, I didn't get Myrtle Beach. But Seymour-Johnson was only a few hours away and I figured that was darned close to what I asked for, especially considering the geography of coming from Japan all the way back to the Carolinas.

During my time in Goldsboro we made it down to Myrtle twice, I think it was, and it was a real blast. Lots of girls, bars and clubs, and live music. I even saw Marvin Gaye live down there. Myrtle lived up to all my images of it. I still like it there and visited it many years later on a solo trip I made back to the Carolinas. Excellent place, with excellent beaches.

Anyway, at Seymour-Johnson, I worked at headquarters of the 4th Tactical Fighter Wing. It was still the military, but except for one annoying technical sergeant, it was a good assignment and was way more professionally administered than the USAFSS had been. The 4th was a showcase wing, with four squadrons of F-4 fighters, and it was run tightly, efficiently, and with considerable pride.

I worked as the clerk for the number two man in the wing, Colonel Turner, and he was an excellent officer, demanding, intense, but fair and, in my case, extremely helpful. My poor behavior in Misawa had stuck me at the rank of E-3 (Airman Second Class) but Colonel Turner personally got me promoted to E-4 (Airman First Class). I will always appreciate him for doing that.

Because the 4th was a more professional organization, I behaved more professionally myself. I worked hard in the 4th and advanced in my new career field (clerk) rapidly and successfully. I made a bunch of new buddies and we shared a lot of new experiences. Now, don't get me wrong. I still drank too much and raised a little too much hell, but I wasn't as bad as I had been in Misawa.

In fact, even though I had been staying out of trouble for the most part, one night me and my buddy Eddie got arrested out in Goldsboro, on this strip of clubs and restaurants outside the main gate to the base. We had gone into a hamburger joint all tanked up and ordered some food. When the kids said they were closed and

wouldn't wait on us, we decided to express our displeasure by refus-
ing to leave until we got our chow.

What we got was arrested by the Goldsboro police. All the way
to the station, Eddie kept yelling at the cop, "What are we, killers?"
The cop was mad but kept his cool. I kept telling Eddie to "shut the
f... up," but he kept up his harangue all the way to the police station.
Suffice it to say, the local gendarmes did not take kindly to Eddie's
behavior and they slapped him around quite a bit with open hands.
Finally, they tossed us in a drunk tank, the two of us in this cell with
metal beds and no pads, blankets, or pillows.

They waited until about two-thirty or three in the morning, it was
a Friday or Saturday night I remember that, to call our unit back on
base to come and get us. I think they were hoping that by calling so
early in the morning it would make our first sergeant mad. He had to
come and get us after all, and we would be in more trouble back on
base. Too bad for them, our first shirt was very lenient and saw this
as no more than some young guys blowing off steam. There's another
guy I owe a big thanks, too, and I don't even remember his name.

The upshot of it all was that Eddie and I had to go downtown
to court and the judge, probably used to GIs acting foolish like this,
dropped the trespassing charge and only made us pay a small fine
for Public Drunkenness. I remember the fine—eight dollars. Not
bad, huh?

Sometime later, maybe only a few weeks, I had one of the defin-
ing moments in my life. It had to do with the only time in my life,
so far, that I've ever had a gun pulled on me. Directly on me. Here's
how that went down.

I was riding in a car with some of my Air Force buddies and
we'd been drinking, what a surprise. We were cruising on the far,
east side of Goldsboro, an area we didn't usually go to, and we got
into a shouting match with a carload of local boys. The upshot was,
they pulled into a grocery store parking lot and so did we, our driver

bringing his car up alongside the left side of theirs. The jawing continued and finally one of them called us out.

I was drunk enough to think I was tough, which I wasn't and never have been (unless buoyed by a large amount of intoxicating spirits, in which case I was still not tough but inclined to get rowdy). So, I got out of my side of the car behind our driver and walked behind the local boys' car and up to the shotgun rider, the one who had called us out. I didn't know what I was going to do as I went up there but the local kid solved that problem for me.

As I reached his door, he swung it open and put a small caliber pistol directly into my stomach. The barrel was pushing against my large and unmilitary-like belly. Luckily for me, I was inebriated enough to not be too scared yet sober enough to not do anything stupid. What I did was stop in my tracks, the pistol had already done that for me, anyway, and then calmly fold my arms against my chest.

Without a word, I slowly began to walk away, backward. Step by step I went, calmly, quietly. When I got back to our car I leaped in and shouted. "He pulled a gun on me. Jesus Christ, the guy put a gun in my gut."

"What?"

"I'm not kidding. Right here. I saw it. I felt it."

"Let's get out of here." Our shotgun rider correctly suggested.

The guy driving slammed our car into reverse and we shot back out of the parking space and prepared to make a hasty exit. To our chagrin, the local boys paralleled our moves from a few feet behind us. We looked back at them to see that the guy with the gun had now gotten into the back, left seat, same as I was in our car, and they were preparing to rush by us. Before we could get going they did exactly that.

We were amazed and more than a little freaked out as the gunner stuck his pistol out the window as they roared by us. We all hollered and ducked down, me and the other guy in the back seat hit the floorboard. As we were ducking, the kid gunner fired off two loud, ringing shots. We yelled again and even louder when the shots seemed to hit the side of the car with us down there in the floorboard. There were two distinct and definite thuds against the back right side of our car. We were sure we had been shot. But we hadn't.

"Blanks." The driver shook his head.

"Blanks." We were all darned glad they had been.

"Let's go get 'em."

I wasn't that keen on the new plan myself because I was getting sober fast and they had a big head start, but we did go after them. It took us a while to locate them but we followed them out of town a little ways until they stopped. We pulled up and started to get out. The gunner kid leaned out from the backseat and pointed the gun at us.

"You were shooting blanks." Our driver pointed at him.

"*Was.* But I loaded it up with live ammo now. Want to try me?"

"He's bluffin'."

"Try me."

"Hell, he could've switched them. It could be real ammunition."

"Good thinking." The kid smiled.

"Screw you."

"I got the pistol."

"Let's go." Our driver let it go for all of us. There was no way to know if the punk had put live ammo in the pistol or not.

So we split. I think we went back to the base and stewed on the experience for a while. After that we didn't go back to that far, eastern part of town anymore. We stayed in the places where GIs mostly hung out. It was a lesson that we learned. For a change.

Freezing My Fanny in Kunsan, Korea

ON JANUARY 23, 1968, THE U.S.S. *Pueblo* was captured by North Korea. Five days after the spy ship was taken, the advance party (including myself) of the 4th Tactical Fighter Wing arrived in Kunsan, Korea. It was cold and dreary there.

In fact, it was super cold in Korea in the winter and the arrival of our entire wing within about ten days or so put severe stress on the little base's resources. The military population went from something like eighteen hundred people to over sixty-five hundred in about two weeks. The Corps of Engineers was soon busy building gigantic tent cities where we enlisted men moved after spending some time in old Quonset huts and overstuffed barracks where the stoves wouldn't stay lit and the water was ice cold coming out of the shower. That was uncomfortable, the icy showers I mean.

I lived in two different tent cities during my five month stay in Kunsan. They weren't all that bad, especially after it started to warm up but at first they were darned nippy. The stoves were gas cans filled with kerosene and they were lit by priming them with a pump and then some kind of lighting mechanism, which I can no longer recall.

What I do remember is that when you first got a new can of kerosene you had to prime it, light it, and stay with it until the heat started coming out. Even working at its best, you can imagine one

Kerosene Heating Oil Storage, Kunsan AB, Korea, February 1968.
Seymour-Johnson AFB Library and Digital Collections

of those cans didn't exactly make the tent feel like summertime. But they were adequate.

I have some vivid memories of those early days in Korea. One night before the tent cities were built, soon after we had arrived, our sergeants rousted us out of the Airman's Club and made us dig these rotting, tearing old tents out of a dumpster that had probably not been opened since the end of the Korean War.

The reason I recall this night is that it was one of the coldest I had ever experienced up to that point in my life. I remember thinking how in the world did the poor GIs survive innumerable nights out in this cold all night long during the war? I wouldn't have been able to move, much less raise my rifle to fight. It made me admire the ones who did even more than I had before.

Several other things happened early in our time in Kunsan at that Airman's Club. On the positive side they had great food, serving these huge cheeseburgers which were called *yobo* burgers (*yobo* was slang for a girl, like moose was in Japan), tasty French fries and small pizzas. Also, I was lucky with the slot machines there and won several jackpots which augmented my bi-monthly paychecks.

On the negative side, an Army kid stationed at some nearby site laid his M-16 against a table in the club and it slipped down and cranked a round off into the ceiling of the club. That caused a new rule. No loaded weapons allowed inside. That was a good rule. The worst thing that happened in the club, however, was really bad.

One night while I was in there playing the slots, the most vicious and violent fight I've ever seen broke out. It was a small scale race riot, a dangerous brawl between black and white Airmen. The slot machines, luckily for me, were in back of the club, and so I managed, barely, too avoid being drug into this foul conflict. One of the black guys in the fight was my friend and tent mate Butch. In a race riot, it doesn't matter who your friends are, the lines are clearly defined. I am so glad I avoided that fight. It still leaves an empty place in me when I remember it.

I can't tell about Kunsan without telling more about the food. We ate a lot of C-rations, which weren't all that bad. The meat was decent and they always had crackers and other small edibles in them that tasted fine. Each ration box or package usually had a four-pack of cigarettes, too, and at the time we all thought that was great. As for the chow hall, however, not so good. Again, it probably wasn't their fault. To quadruple the number of people you had to feed in only a couple of weeks' time had to tax the system big time.

Mostly what I remember about the chow hall were the powdered eggs. You could put all the catsup in the world on those eggs and they never tasted right or good. Like I did at most of my bases, I ended up frequently buying my own food at whatever snack bar was available. That's the way life was there.

One final note about life on TDY (Temporary Duty) to Kunsan. The base BX (Base Exchange, like a small department store, sort of) was always running out of basic goods, like cigarettes. It was at least partly because of the increase in demand, but also because of supply people selling GI goods to the off base black market for a profit. Oops, who would have ever heard of such a thing.

We used to pay fourteen cents a pack for filter smokes and twelve cents for non-filters. At one point, the supply had dropped down to only two brands of unfiltered smokes, Lucky Strikes and Chesterfields. Now, my mom smoked Lucky's her whole life, but they were too strong for me so I went for the Chesterfields, not a heck of a lot better or smoother I'll tell you. We griped about the scarcity of smokes but what could you do?

What you could do was go downtown into Kunsan city and buy any kind of American cigarette that you wanted. Yes, sir, the old black market. It exists outside every base of ours that I've ever heard of in the world. For the then outrageous price of thirty-five cents a pack, we could by whatever brand we wanted down in the bars in Kunsan.

We griped about that, but we coughed up the money (so to speak) to get our favorite cigarettes. When you wanted a Winston or a Marlboro, well, you didn't have much choice. It was buy them downtown when you were there or do without. It was a simple system. Everyone knew how it worked and we all used it. That's the way that kind of thing works. Simple and straightforward.

Helping Chuck Yeager
Serve Coffee to Generals

TO TELL MY Chuck Yeager story I have to backtrack a little. First of all, the only reason I have a Chuck Yeager story to tell at all is because right about the time my fighter wing unit got sent over to Korea we lost our long-time commander, a gruff but decent old guy who only had a sixth-grade education. We were commander-less as we prepared to go to Kunsan and I saw an interesting battle over who would command our advance party and the wing while we waited on our new commander.

My colonel, Colonel Turner, who was second in command to begin with, won this battle. As I recall, he had like one day time in grade over another full colonel and so was entitled to command the unit. This struggle for leadership was interesting to be around. I mean it went down to the wire until Colonel Turner's records showed clearly that he had the other colonel beat.

As noted in the previous section, I was part of the Advon (advance) party going over with the first one hundred men, enlisted and officers. I remember sitting in this big C-141 transport jet rigged up with a bunch of rows of seats facing backward toward the tail of the aircraft. Colonel Turner was either immediately on my left or only one or two seats away.

We flew directly from Seymour-Johnson to Elmendorf AFB in

Alaska (landing in a blizzard), then on to Yokota Air Base, Japan, before making the final leg into Kunsan AB, Korea. For the first few weeks, about a month as I recall, wing headquarters operated out of an underground bunker (we were preparing for war against North Korea) and then we moved into a small HQ building that was sandbagged all around up to about chest height.

I don't know why, but Colonel Turner left right away when we got to Korea. He went to the War College back in D.C., I think. I bet he made general somewhere along the way. Anyway, the part of our above ground HQ that concerned me on a day-to-day work basis was the area directly inside the building where the communications center (Comm Center) was. My buddies Danny and Tony manned it. Toward the left and set back was a rectangular area where the commander and his second in command had their offices. This was where I worked.

During the command transition, Lt. Colonel Damewood, who was always good to work for, replaced Colonel Turner as the number two man. I was his clerk and Art, another of my buddies, was the commander's clerk. When you walked through an open doorway into our area, I was ahead and slightly to the right with Colonel Damewood's office in another room to the right of that. On the left, also in a separate small area was Art, and left of him the commander's office.

That was the general layout. There were a couple more desks out where I was and some large cabinets filled with classified material which yours truly was supposed to destroy in the event of an enemy attack. We had an incendiary grenade for that purpose. I was assigned anything that had to do with highly classified material because of my Top Secret clearance from my USAFSS days.

I also worked with two sergeants, Satterfield and Byrd (the latter of whom I still owe an apology, for rudeness, after all these years), and Major Turk, Colonel Damewood's adjutant and the flight ops officer, who was in the office a lot as well. In fact, part of my job was

Colonel Chuck Yeager officially taking command of the 4th Tactical Fighter Wing at Kunsan AB, Korea, March 1968.

Seymour-Johnson AFB Library and Digital Collections

to drive one of the jeeps over to the officer hootches (small houses) and bring Major Turk to HQ each morning. We developed a solid working relationship and Major Turk not only explained fighter wing mission and tactical information to me but ended up signing my application to enter the University of Nebraska when I got out of the service. Now that was a good officer there.

Back to my Chuck Yeager story. Shortly after we got to Korea and Colonel Turner left for parts not fully known, Colonel Chuck Yeager arrived in Kunsan to command the 4th Tactical Fighter Wing. Colonel Yeager was a straight shooting, down to earth man. He treated everyone well and we all liked him. We had a nickname for him, though, the Phantom. And not because, like all the other pilots, he flew an F-4 Phantom jet.

We called him the phantom because he was out of the area a lot. It was believed that he liked pheasant hunting on Okinawa and flew down there frequently to pursue his hobby. Wherever he went, when he came back he was as good a commander as you're going to get.

One of these times when the colonel was around, we had some sort of major honcho meeting there in Kunsan in Colonel Damewood's office, as I recall, although I don't remember him being there. At any rate, we had either eight or nine generals, brigadier and above, in that room. HQ was lousy with stars. There were even one or two three-star generals, I'm certain of that.

For me, it was a terrifying experience. I had seen generals at our HQ in North Carolina but they were usually alone, one at a time. This was eight or nine in one place and they were some major players. The head of the Fifth Army, I think it was, was there, some hotshot Air Force guy from the big base up in Osan, and a PACAF (Pacific Air Force Command) honcho from Japan, too—that sort of thing. I was afraid one of these guys would look up at me and see what a screw up I was and bust me down to Airman Basic right on the spot. Of course, the truth was, they didn't even see me I was so insignificant to them.

So there we were, me, Art, and Chuck Yeager and a room full of big shot generals. Holy cow. You want to know what kind of guy Chuck Yeager was? This man, the man who broke the speed of sound, the importance of which cannot be diminished in any way, this man, his clerk Art, my bud, and me, the beer bellied little E-4 who was finally getting short in the service but was still scared to death in front of all that brass, the three of us served coffee to that covey of commanders. Amazing. Two enlisted guys and one of the greatest test pilots, if not the greatest, in history, serving coffee like we were working in the chow hall.

That's my Chuck Yeager story. The main thing I remember from it is that Colonel Yeager (who eventually made Brigadier General himself) never once acted like he was somebody more important than me or Art, and we both knew he was, big time. It's a testament to the man, if you ask me. He was down to earth, a real person. If you ever saw him on TV, he was exactly as he appeared. Straight ahead and honest. It was cool working for him and I'm glad I did.

You're Exactly What's Wrong with America Today, Boy

BY LATE SPRING 1968, I was getting short. That is, I had only about three months or so until my four year enlistment would be over. I was ready to get out. I was tired of being in the service. Somewhere around in there, me and a couple of my buds from HQ got a major break. Colonel Damewood, maybe at Major Turk's instigation, let me and my pals take a three-day R&R to Japan. That was an excellent deal.

I'll never forget the ride over to Tachikawa Air Base in a C-130 cargo plane. First of all, the E-4 (they were calling us Sergeant by then even though most of us were uncomfortable with that new designation) couldn't believe the orders we handed him when we boarded the C-130.

"There's no destination on here." He was incredulous and gave our orders a close reading.

"It's classified." One of my buds explained to him, which was the truth. "Nobody's supposed to know we're even here."

"Not exactly per regulation."

"Nothing we do is."

"Well, climb on in and find somewhere to sit. We're not set up for troop transport."

"No sweat."

"We could get a military hop anywhere in the world with these orders." My other buddy climbed on board. "Anywhere."

"Cool." I anticipated three days of drinking and carousing in the environs of Tokyo out the backside of Tachikawa. Back to Japan for me. I had been gone just over a year from my Misawa assignment.

At the time, Tachikawa was the hub for all travel in the Orient. It was a revolving door of soldiers, marines, sailors, and airmen traveling to and from Japan, Korea, Viet Nam, Thailand, and so on. It was busy all the time but had a laid back atmosphere because nobody was involved in military work there, except for base personnel. It was way more relaxed than other bases. I always liked being at Tachi.

So we flew over to Japan in the C-130. I rode most of the way sitting on equipment that was chained down on that big door that opens up in back of the plane. I enjoyed the ride. After our three day bash, we drank in the bars, we gambled, we drank, we stuffed ourselves with snack bar food, and we drank. And we headed back to Korea on a commercial jet when it was over.

On the job again, I found that instead of the R&R making me relaxed and feeling good, it was the opposite. I was angry all the time, short with the sergeants I worked with, grumpy to the extreme. I simply didn't want to be in the military anymore and I couldn't stand the idea of even three little old months to go. That seemed like an eternity. I wanted out now.

One day, maybe a Friday, we had some new procedure come down for getting passes to downtown Kunsan City. We had to go into a room off to the side of the Comm Center where our sergeants were at desks giving lectures about how to behave downtown before they handed out the passes.

Well, this struck me as a lot of bull. I could not and would not put up with a lecture about running the bars and alleys of Kunsan when we'd already been doing it for a couple of months by then. With that short timer's chip on my shoulder and a bad case of burn-out (although we didn't use that term yet), I went in to get my pass. Unfortunately, the sergeant designated to give us the lecture and then the pass was my own Sergeant Byrd.

He didn't have any choice. It was a dictate from somewhere on high. So there I was, standing in front of Sergeant Byrd and he began the lecture. He didn't get two words out before I went off.

"Give me the pass or not." I was stupidly rude. "I don't want to hear no lecture."

Now there was no reason for me to act that way, but I was in this crappy short-timer's mood after Tachi and so I acted like a complete jerk. This is why I still owe Sergeant Byrd an apology because I never did apologize to him over there.

I paid for my little outburst, though. With pass in hand, minus the lecture, I walked back out into the hallway by the Comm Center and directly into instant Karma hell. A master sergeant, one I had never seen before and would never see again, had witnessed my exchange with my sergeant and he was ready to ream me out, which he did.

"You." He growled, pointed his finger at me like it was a pistol.

I didn't say anything back and would have walked on, but he was right on me.

"What the hell's the matter with you? Who do you think you are? I ought to pull that pass right now."

I remained motionless in front of the angry master sergeant, angry myself but not speaking.

"You're a fine one. And look at that hair. It's a disgrace. You know what's the matter with you, boy? You're exactly what's wrong with America today. You're spoiled, and you don't have any respect for authority. Well, I'm going to show you some. Now get your ass over to the barbershop and get that haircut. I mean right now."

I still didn't say anything. I couldn't. I was shaking and as mad as I could possibly be, but I knew I could not react to this master sergeant. My fanny would be in a ringer if I did. I had had a face-off with one of our technical sergeants back in Carolina, a real martinet, right up to the point where he was about to charge me with insubordination. I finally lost that confrontation, too. Visions of the brig always won out.

"You get a haircut." The master sergeant repeated, yelled at me. "And when you're done, you report back to me. Do you understand? Do you, boy?"

I grunted something that could be taken as an affirmative to that question but I was so mad myself that I didn't dare say anything directly to him. I knew I would only get myself in bigger trouble if I did. I would have a serious problem if I back talked this guy.

So, in impotent rage, I went back to my office, which was across the big hallway, and went back to work, upset, frustrated, angry. I discussed the situation with Art and Danny and Tony, who came in to see me after the dust up. I was adamant that I wasn't going to do anything the lousy master sergeant ordered me to. They shook their heads in commiseration. But they knew, as I did, that I couldn't win in this situation. After a half hour or maybe forty-five minutes, I tucked my tail between my legs and, out of fear of a real confrontation with my superiors, went over to the BX barbershop and got a haircut.

I did not look for the master sergeant after I did, however. There was no way I was going to report back to him. He could forget that part. The haircut was as far as I would go. And nothing else ever came of it. I never saw him again and I did not present myself and my new haircut to anyone for their approval or disapproval. The whole thing faded away, probably luckily for me.

It all faded with one exception. The unavoidable fact that I had treated Sergeant Byrd poorly. I lost his friendship and our working relationship was ice cold all the way up to my return to the states. I never saw him again after that and that's why I say I still owe him an apology. I suppose, after all this time, it doesn't matter anymore, but this is my apology anyway. Better late than never. Hopefully.

Lights Out,
Gimme an M-16

INTELLIGENCE REPORTS WERE always crossing my desk at HQ warning us that we were going to get overrun by enemy forces. Kunsan was relatively too far south for such a thing to happen, but I kept that information in the back of my mind anyway. I've never been the hero type, but I wanted to be ready for such an eventuality no matter how unlikely its occurrence. About two months or so into our TDY, with these concerns about being overrun at least somewhere in the back of my mind, an incident occurred that got me all worked up.

One night we were working a swing shift, we didn't do a whole lot of shift work but we often manned HQ around the clock so somebody had to be there, and things were going slow. It was probably about eight p.m., and with not much work to do, I had been visiting with Danny and Tony out in the Comm Center. I had just walked back into my office area when all of a sudden, and without any kind of warning, all the power on the base died. I mean it shut down. Lights out.

The absolute first thing that went through my mind were those reports. *This is it,* I thought, *they are going to try to overrun the base. Holy crap!* I was supposed to find that incendiary grenade and be ready to burn all our records if something like this happened but that was secondary to me. Number one on my agenda was self-protection.

The first thing I wanted to do was find me an M-16 and some ammo, and there was only one of them around HQ. It was out in the Comm Center with Tony and Danny. They had an M-16 and one clip of ammo. I headed straight for the Comm Center.

"You got that M-16?"

"We got it."

"Let me have that son of a gun. I ain't got no weapon."

"No way." Tony held tightly to the M-16. He and Danny knew about the reports, too.

I didn't know what to do exactly, there wasn't even so much as a sergeant there at HQ, but I knew I wanted to be armed. Danny and Tony at least had one M-16. I wanted one badly.

"Come on, guys."

"Get your own."

"There ain't any more, Tony. Come on."

"Nothin' doin'."

"Hell."

The base was pitch black, we had no idea why. North Koreans could be storming us any second now. We had no way of knowing.

For the next quarter of an hour or so, I stayed in my office area, looking for the incendiary grenade, I couldn't find that either, and worrying. I hated not having anything to defend myself with. I didn't have so much as a flashlight to help me search for the burn grenade for crying out loud.

Then, about the time I was considering going outside HQ to try and locate some kind of weapon or protection or something, the power booted back up. There was that *whoomp* sound that you hear when the big power grids come back online and then the lights all over the base came back on as well. It had been a simple power drop. A black out. Nothing more.

No North Korean invaders.

Still, the next day I was a little skittish yet. I went straight to Sgt.

Satterfield and demanded that I be given an M-16 of my own for future exigencies. He thought that was funny.

"You sure are a jumpy little fart, arent' you?" He wrote off both my reaction to the previous night's event and my request with a laugh.

"I'm serious."

"It was a black out. Nothing more."

"It could have been something."

"But it wasn't." Yet he relented a little. "Go ahead and check with the squadron commander and see if he'll authorize you a weapon. If it matters so much to you."

"All right."

Later in the day, I went to the squadron commander, a weird little lieutenant whose only contact with me had been after my run in with the Goldsboro police when my friend Eddie and I had been arrested for trespassing and public drunkenness. The guy was basically an incompetent, hiding in a trivial job. Everything that mattered took place at the wing level, not the squadron level.

He explained that he couldn't authorize me an M-16. I don't remember what ridiculous reason he gave but there was nothing I could do about it. On top of that, I found out that the ammo for the M-16s he did have was kept somewhere down on the flight line a mile or more away from HQ. For crying out loud. Sgt. Satterfield laughed again when I came back and detailed my attempt to get an M-16.

"I need something in here, Sarge." I whined. "Couldn't I at least get a big flashlight or something so that I could see?"

He just looked up at me and shook his head. This was all silliness to him. I was overreacting. It was only a power outage. No need to change the way things were done. No need for extra weapons or flashlights.

As usual, the military way won over any personal concerns I might have had. And in this case it didn't matter. We never did have another power failure like that and, of course, the North Koreans never came close to overrunning Kunsan, but small, guerrilla groups did infiltrate the south up closer to the DMZ from time to time.

I still thought they should have let me be prepared. It was the military after all and we were sandbagged in for war. It didn't seem to me that being ready for the unexpected was such a laughable thing. But then again, the military and I seldom saw eye to eye on things. I was quite familiar with that by then and my time in the service was coming mercifully to an end.

Battleship in HQ, Getting the Heck Out

I WENT TO KOREA in the advance party and because I was getting short with about a month to go before being discharged, I got to come home early, well ahead of the rest of the fighter wing. Seymour-Johnson Air Force Base was almost completely deserted, at least the TAC (Tactical Air Command) side was. There was absolutely nothing for me to do.

There was one enlisted guy in HQ who had somehow managed to not get sent to Korea and he and I whiled away our days putting pages into military manuals and twiddling our thumbs. Finally, one of us came up with the idea of bringing in the board game Battleship to combat our boredom (pun intended). It was great. For the last three weeks of my military hitch, I played Battleship, over and over. We sat at my desk in HQ and sank each other's ships again and again and again. It was quite a bit of fun.

The only other thing I had to do during this time was begin the mustering out process. Despite having received a letter in Korea saying I was a non-selectee for re-enlistment, when it came time for me to see the re-up guy (just some airman with no more rank than me) he asked me if I wanted to re-enlist.

At Kunsan, with the help of Colonel Damewood and Major Turk, I had fought the non-selectee status, not because I wanted to

Receiving award from Col. Damewood, Kunsan AB, Korea, March 1968
J. B. Hogan Collection

stay in, but because the reason they gave was false—they said I had not advanced in my work specialty. It was a peculiar reason since I had not only advanced in my original specialty, Morse Intercept Operator, but cross-trained and advanced as a Clerk Typist as well. In achieving skilled levels in not just one but in two specialties, I had done something very few one-term airmen ever do. Take that Air Force. On some level, however, they must've been desperate.

Now, some of my sergeants liked to joke with me that I had no chance outside. That was what we always said that NCO stood for, not non-commissioned officer, but no chance outside in the real, civilian world. The sergeants often said to me: "Hogan, you better stay in. You have zero chance of succeeding in the civilian world." Despite their admonitions and the incorrect labeling of me as a non-selectee for re-enlistment which we had gotten corrected in Korea, when it came time to sign those re-up papers which the young airman presented to me, I firmly signed the not going to re-enlist option and instead signed the papers that freed me from active duty.

On my way home on the day I got out, two things happened that I never forgot. One of which I always regretted as well. First of all, I got bumped from a standby flight at Newport News, Virginia. On my last day in the service, I got bumped off a flight for the first and only time in the entire four years. That was remarkable right there. I finally caught a quick flight up to D.C. and from there to Cleveland and on to Chicago's Midway Airport.

It was at Midway that I did the thing that I later came to regret. I took all my military clothes out of my duffle bag and threw them into a big trash receptacle. The only thing I kept that was military were my brogans. I wore them until they fell off my feet.

Why did it matter later that I threw away those meaningless Air Force uniforms? Well, first of all, in barely more than a year I would be wearing the fatigue shirts again as a fashion statement. Everybody in college wore them in those days, and I could've been wearing my own instead of buying one out of an Army surplus store with some other guy's last name sewed on it. Duh. Oh, well.

What I shouldn't have thrown away, though, even though it no longer fit me nor would it ever again, was my beautiful blue winter dress coat. It was the Air Force's blue version of the Navy peacoat, only way prettier and much more stylish. Somebody could have gotten some use out of that coat. It was a thing of beauty. Too bad.

But I tossed it and all the rest of my military clothing right there in the trash bin at Midway Airport. It was July 12, 1968, my mustering out day, and I didn't care about fashion or beauty or anything else. All I knew was that I had finally completed my four-year hitch and that I was a civilian once more. Those uniforms were yesterday's news and I wanted nothing more to do with them. It was only in hindsight that I later regretted tossing the unis and stuff.

They say hindsight, particularly historical hindsight, is twenty-twenty. Well, that may be true, but sometimes you simply act in the moment and don't give a darn how you may feel about it later. That's the way I felt that day, anyway. All I wanted was to be discharged, and I was.

I was out. I was free. I was a civilian again. That was all I cared about. I didn't give a darn about anything else. I had done my time, not so well I'm sure, but that was all behind me now. I wasn't Sergeant E-4 Hogan anymore, I was Jerry B. Hogan, Civilian First Class. So long, Air Force. Thank you very much.

Readjustment Blues

DON'T LET ANYBODY tell you that a GI doesn't go through the readjustment blues, even when he hasn't been in a war zone. I sure as heck did, and it lasted all the way through my first year out, a year I spent going to the University of Nebraska in Lincoln, and beyond.

To begin with, although I was newly twenty-three years old, I felt decades older than my fellow students. While they were studying toward their degrees, engaging in social life on campus, going to sporting events, or demonstrating against the war or lousy campus administrations, I had been living the life of a drunken degenerate. I felt world weary and disconnected. I drifted through that year, trying to find my civilian legs but failing completely. The only things I managed to do that extremely forgettable year were give baseball one last try and finally, after trying about four other areas, settle on English as my major. I tried business the first semester and it was so boring it drove me into the literature classes where I finally understood I belonged.

As for baseball, I was in terrible shape. I smoked like a chimney and still drank to excess too frequently. I could barely make it around the track when I walked on with NU's baseball team, but I did play well. I hit and fielded well and thought I might have a shot despite my lack of conditioning. I didn't.

Shortly after the two available walk-on positions on the baseball team were filled by two kids who didn't even go through the tryout with the rest of us, at least twenty to twenty-five guys, I decided greener pastures awaited me. I applied to and was accepted at Central Missouri State down in Warrensburg, Missouri. The fall of 1969 would find me well south of Lincoln and ready for a new lease on life. Luckily for me, that's exactly what was awaiting.

How I Learned Every Street in Every Town in North Central Missouri

WELL, MAYBE THAT title is a bit of an exaggeration, but in the summer of 1969, I learned a heck of a lot of streets in a bunch of towns in north central Missouri. Before heading farther south to Warrensburg, I was staying with my middle brother Joe in Chillicothe, doing occasional odd jobs that popped up. For a while I worked for a moving company and made decent money at that but like most of my jobs it was short term.

When I wasn't working that summer, I went swimming and played fast pitch softball for a local team. Then finally, not long after the astronauts set foot on the moon, I landed a job here on terra firma delivering soap samples in the little towns all around the area.

The bag of samples was heavy when you first started a load but it lightened up quickly as you dropped off box after box of the detergent on porches, front steps and, if the dog was big or scary enough, out in the front yard. Because we were on foot, we literally did learn practically every street and I still have a feeling of belonging to that part of Missouri and to those little towns.

There was Chillicothe, of course, where we started and then we moved on to the east, quickly covering Laclede (near where John J. Pershing was born), and then Brookfield (where I also played well in a regional fast pitch softball tournament that summer) and Marceline.

I also remember doing Trenton and finally we ended up in Carrolton down by the Missouri River.

We walked up and down the streets. Through the neighborhoods. Around the small downtowns. In the suburbs. Out on the edge of town. Up and down, back and forth. Dusty, hot, sweaty. Looking up at the street signs for Broadway or Main, practically every town in America has a Broadway and a Main, and then the Maples, Oaks, Jeffersons, Washingtons, and on and on and on, ad infinitum. It was repetitive but it was personal. You got to know those little towns and I'm still glad I did that, heat and dirt and sweat and all.

As I recall, that summer was also Reggie Jackson's rookie year in the major leagues and he was bashing homerun after homerun, which we listened to on a transistor radio somebody had in the van when we went back for more samples, for breaks, and for lunch. It was hot and dusty and tiring hauling the samples around but the worst part for me was dealing with all the stupid dogs people had.

Oddly enough, the only real trouble I had was not with big dogs, like German Shepherds or Doberman Pinschers, but with little ones. Yappy, snappy, annoying little rat dogs. One day in Trenton they finally got me. I went up to this house and the two little mutts, I don't even remember what breed they were, if any recognizable one, started circling me, yapping their stupid heads off.

I kicked at them and yelled and tried to get past them, but they were intent on hassling me. Finally, they pulled a tricky little maneuver on me. While I was busy kicking at one of them, the other one sneaked around behind me and bit right into the lower part of my right calf through my jeans. It didn't hurt that much but it made me mad. I kicked and yelled at the little dogs until they finally ran away.

When my supervisor found out I had been bit, he hurried up to check my wound. It wasn't much more than a little skin broken (in the shape of the dumb little dog's teeth bite) but there was some blood. I think we put a small bandage on it and let it go at that. It did get me the rest of the afternoon off, with pay. That was a cool thing. I got to sit in the air-conditioned van and loaf until the rest of the day's samples were delivered. Easy money. I was back at work the next day and continued delivering samples until the company finished saturating that part of Missouri and moved on.

I could have gone with them but they were headed for New Jersey and I didn't want to go there when I was getting ready to start attending Central Missouri State College at the end of the summer. So, I managed to land a hot, sawdusty job at a local lumber yard. They wanted me to stay on, too, but I was ready to bail. It was time to go to Warrensburg and begin my second year of college after getting out of the Air Force. Toward the latter part of August 1969 that is exactly what I did.

Drinking Purple Passion Out of a Plastic Trash Can Is No Way to Start a School Year

IN LATE AUGUST of 1969, I hitchhiked from Chillicothe to Warrensburg to take up residence in the latter town and attend Central Missouri State College (later Central Missouri State University and now the University of Central Missouri). I got a ride all the way from Chillicothe to Sedalia with two older couples cruising around central Missouri in their RV.

They were fine folks. The man driving said they picked me up because I was carrying my belongings in a laundry bag which he thought was maybe a Navy bag. It was still okay when he found out the bag was Air Force issue. As long as I was an ex-GI, he was okay with that.

These people were so nice that when they stopped halfway down, I can't remember where anymore, they fed me right along with them. That was a particularly decent thing to do, and I thanked them several times. Finally, they dropped me off at Wheel-In, a drive-in restaurant on the northwest corner of the four-way intersection where Highway 65 (running north-south) and Highway 50 (running east-west) cross one another in west Sedalia.

I thanked the friendly folks, got a soda and French fries at the Wheel-In, and after a not too long wait hitched another ride over to Warrensburg with a college kid driving a cool little sports car. It was later in the afternoon when I walked up the sidewalk to the house that would be my home for the next year. 209 E. Market Street. There's nothing but an empty lot there now, or there was the last time I was in Warrensburg, but at the time it was a grand old house.

That first afternoon when I walked into the house I had no idea that the coming year would be one of momentous change for me, a time of growth, pain, joy and, essentially, re-birth. There were about eight or ten other guys renting rooms in the big house besides me. Perk, Altie, Russ, Billy, Marv, and Walt among them. Most of us would become fast friends and the ones who did are still friends to this day.

209 E. Market was a two-story home owned by the son of a local shoe store owner and it had been converted into rooms that were rented to older male students. In those days, the older male students were frequently veterans and that is exactly what all of us were. Except for Marv's room, all of the rooms were set up for two people, almost like my Air Force barracks rooms in that sense. I shared my room with Walt, a big, gruff, blast of a guy from Kansas City.

When you came into the house, my and Walt's room was on the immediate right. To the immediate left was the stairs leading up to the second floor. There were three two-man rooms up there, Marv's one-man room, and a large bathroom. Inside the downstairs door, angled slightly across from my room was, of all things, a pay telephone with a small chair and table in a kind of alcove if you will. Down the hallway on the left was Russ and Billy's room. In back of the house was a big kitchen and an International Harvester refrigerator (the only one of that brand I've ever seen) which we all shared, although we kept private areas within it for our personal food.

Back up by my room and to the right was a large living room and off to the side of it a small bathroom. The living room was the social center of the house. We would sit out there in a couple of big, comfortable chairs or on the couch and BS, watch TV, play music, or

Post-Air Force, sitting on front porch, Warrensburg, MO, 1969-1970.
Photo by Steve Perkins

sometimes all of them at once. In early 1970, when we started smoking a lot of weed we tended to congregate in the living room and sit
stoned out of our minds listening to Hendrix, Leonard Cohen, Joe
Cocker, or Crosby, Stills, Nash and Young with the TV on and the
sound off. Those were great, mellow times.

One of the most extraordinary things about the living room was
what we did to its huge floor made of some dark wood. Being ex-
GIs, none of us was too fastidious and since we all smoked still, this
was before we fretted so much about smoking, we would toss our
cigarette butts down on the floor and stamp them out. There were
so many burnt spots on it that the floor looked like the pockmarked
face of the moon. I swear. It was unbelievable.

Anyway, the first night I spent in the house (my brother Joe had
driven me down from Chillicothe a week or ten days before when I
had found the room for rent) I walked into the kitchen in back and
there was Marv mixing grain alcohol with Hawaiian Punch in a huge
plastic trash can. We introduced ourselves and then I asked him what
he called his concoction.

"Purple passion." He let me know there was a party later to which
I was automatically invited.

"Sounds potent." I peered into the can.

"Oh, yeah. It'll catch up on you if you aren't careful.

The party was in an open field our landlord owned on the south
end of town. He gave these little parties in the hope of picking off a
stray, drunk coed. There were a handful of cars parked in a semi-circle
around a large open fire. We, my housemates, friends, and other students, strangers to me, sat around the fire rapping (that meant having
a conversation back in the 60s).

I figured Marv had been kidding about the purple passion so I
was tossing it down quickly. Sometime well after dark, after several
paper cups of this concoction, I decided to stand up and get a refill.
Well, old Marv was right. The purple passion did sneak up on me. I

remember standing up and then everything became wobbly like I was in a Southern California earthquake or something.

I staggered over toward the big plastic trash can with the booze and managed to fill my cup. On the way back to where I'd been chatting with a cute girl and some guy who wouldn't go away, I weaved off to one side and bashed the crap out of my right shin against the grill of one of the parked cars. I scraped it, but good.

"Crap."

"What's the matter?" The cute girl put a hand up to help steady me.

"Nothin'." I didn't want to look like the juiced idiot I was.

"He's drunk." The unwanted boy made points at my expense.

"I'm fine."

Marv came over then to give me a little good-natured bull himself.

"I warned you it would sneak up on you."

"Good stuff." I admitted. Marv was a Nam combat vet and my new housemate and friend. Teasing from him I could take.

Unfortunately for me, Unwanted Boy had apparently scored enough points at my expense, or more likely I was too inebriated to score any myself, that later in the evening he and the cute girl vanished into the soft, Missouri August night. Somewhere around midnight the party broke up and I rode back to 209 E. Market Street with Marv.

Next morning I woke with a terrible hangover. My new roommate Walt had arrived and had some fun banging around the room while putting up his belongings and happily contributing to the sharp pain of my self-inflicted headache.

Fortunately, I didn't have to go to school until sometime around ten a.m. so I was able to put most of the hangover behind me before I presented myself for the first time to my new school. All I had to do was register for some late classes, so it wasn't too bad. Afterward, I began to feel halfway normal and straggled back to Market Street to rest and visit with my new buddies.

"Ready for round two?" Marv was in the kitchen again when I came in later that afternoon. He held up an empty bottle of grain alcohol and pointed at an unused can of Hawaiian Punch.

"Don't think so. Not quite yet."

"Some way to start a new semester at a new school, huh?" He tossed the empty bottle into a trash can.

"Yeah, some way all right."

Marv laughed. I shuffled out of the kitchen and back to my room. I needed a nap.

A Serious Butt Whippin' Sure Does Adjust Your Attitude

EARLY IN THE fall of 1969, in protest (my first one) of the VA getting my GI Bill checks messed up, I started letting my beard and hair grow. I was ready for change that year. I was so tired of the person I'd become while in the service that a kind of personal rebirth was almost a necessity, and maybe not just an 'almost.'

Life at 209 E. Market had continued apace during the fall and early winter. The atmosphere at the house took on an almost communal air. We hung together, drank together, partied together. And some of the parties at the house were extraordinary. At least two of them were so big that the whole house was filled with people, friends from school, a few locals, lots of women.

We all settled into our life of month to month living on GI checks. I learned how to live, for example, on about seven or eight dollars' worth of groceries a week. Life at CMS was fun despite an administration that was reactionary enough to give Attila the Hun a run for his money. Most of us figured out what we needed to get by, grade-wise, and we spent the better part of our time goofing off.

Winter came and I was beginning to look like a freak. My scraggly beard was fully grown out, and my hair was starting to climb over my collar and onto the back of my shoulders. Not especially long, but long enough to separate me from the Joe Straights of the world.

Being weird.
Photo by Thomas Altvater

Everything was going along swimmingly until one Friday night in mid to late February. That's when I had a major encounter downtown with some redneck fraternity boys. Unlike the Hollywood movies, your average guy doesn't win a fight with a pack of other guys. I sure didn't anyway. This is how it went down.

Things, as I implied, were going along comfortably at the house. We were all readjusting together, having fun together, growing together, and then I had the fight. It was a doozy, one of those odd experiences where you could sense something was going to happen but are powerless to stop it, anyway.

I remember leaving the house with Russell and having this nervous, feverish sort of feeling as we walked downtown in the cold night air.

"I feel weird." I recall saying that as we got near the courthouse on our way to Barney's, one of our favorite local watering holes.

"You are weird." Russell joked. "We're all weird, dude. Haven't you learned that yet?"

"I feel funny."

"Couple a cold ones will take care of that, my man."

"Sure, that'll do the trick."

When we came into Barney's out of the chill night air, my roommate Walt was shooting eight-ball at a table near the bar and intimidating his opponent, a better shooter, into losing.

"Hey, roomie." I pointed at him.

Walt nodded, then sidled up next to the kid he was playing and loudly proclaimed he would bet him a hundred bucks the guy couldn't make his next shot. Of course the kid declined the bet but he was so distracted by Walt's aggressiveness he missed a straight shot in the side. Russell and I laughed and went on down the bar.

The place was crowded and loud music, in those days it always seemed to be "Whole Lotta Love" or "Honky Tonk Women," boomed out of the juke box. We struggled to get to the back of the bar where we found Billy who had managed to occupy and hold a table by himself. We waved at him as we cleared the main part of the crowd, which was a pack of fraternity boys slumming at Barney's.

Even after a few beers, and a lot of BS'ing, I was still feeling funky but had settled down some. After I finished my third or fourth beer, I went up to the bar to get a refill and that was when the first salvo of what for me would be a hellish night occurred. I had to work my way through the frat boys to get to a bartender and apparently they didn't like that, at least one of them didn't.

"Hey." A tough looking, flat-eyed guy yelled at me. "Watch what you're doin', hippie."

I was still trying to figure out what the deal was and maybe come up with an apology when I pushed on past the flat-eyed guy toward the bar. But then, without warning, boom, he hit me. I don't remember going down. The next thing I know I'm struggling to my feet and trying to swing at somebody, anybody. Walt was suddenly there, helping me get squared away and I'm asking him what happened.

"C'mon." He aimed me outside. He wasn't brash and bullying now, he was helping.

"Thanks, man." We stood on the sidewalk in front of Barney's. "Somebody hit me."

"No kidding. But you're all right?"

"Who was it?" I was still groggy and a little wobbly on my feet.

About then Billy and Russell burst out of Barney's and rushed up to us.

"Let's take him back to the house." Walt told them. "He's had enough fun for one night."

I went with the guys without much of a struggle though I made some noise about going back in after the guy who hit me. Back at the house we all congregated in the living room and jabbered about what happened.

"Best leave it alone." Walt advised. "Stay here and forget about it."

"Forget about what?" Ruthie, a fun friend who hung with us a lot and even lived at the place for a while, popped in from the kitchen through a door that led into a back sort of anteroom that was part of the living room.

"Some guy hit him down at Barney's." Billy pointed at me. I didn't even have so much as a red place on my face.

"Really!"

Russ and Billy related the details while Walt disappeared into the bathroom near where we stood. Ruthie didn't see that the fight should be any reason to ruin the rest of a Friday night.

"You go down there again." Walt warned me, zipping up his pants as he came out of the bathroom. "You're a fool. You're on your own. Count me out of any of that bull."

"Oh, baloney." Ruthie shook him off. "Walt's an old worry wart."

"Go then." Walt threw up his hands. "I got nothing more to do with it."

And so we went back downtown. I don't know why. I've never known why. The only thing that seems to make sense, a theory I worked out much later, was that I was working out some delayed negative Karma of some kind. Making up for, or paying for, all the crappy things I'd done up to that point in my life. At least all the crazed, wild, drunken stuff I'd pulled off in the service, anyway.

And so we went back downtown. But not to Barney's. Instead we went to another bar called the Church or some such thing, which was another student hangout a couple of blocks away. Of course, almost the first person I see in the bar is the guy who had hit me earlier at Barney's. Naturally.

And again, I don't know why I did what I did but I went straight back to where he sat at the bar. I've never understood why. Perhaps it was some residual sense of meeting a challenge to my manhood. Maybe I still had enough beer in me to be brave, or stupid. Either way, I went directly up to the guy and asked him a most ridiculous question.

"Are you the guy that hit me in Barney's?"

"Yeah." He turned toward me.

"Why did you—" I began.

The guy didn't bother listening for the rest of my next question. He suddenly spun and started to throw a right hand at me. Instinctively, without thinking, I blocked his punch with my left hand and fired a right at him with all my might. Then another, and another. The flat-eyed guy disappeared somewhere into his crowd of frat buddies and then all hell broke loose. The whole pack was on me.

With my back to the bar, I fought a war of attrition I could not win. Throwing right after right at the mob that attacked me, for some reason I never used my left, I took a fearful pounding. Fists were hitting me everywhere, popping into my face in a steady barrage. I don't know how long this went on, but without warning one of the bartenders decided to take a hand. For me it was a hard hand indeed.

Occupied as I was, I had no idea the bartender was coming over the bar behind me. He held a short, lead-filled club, a blackjack. And although I never saw him do it, only felt it, he hit me twice with that sapper. The first hit whacked against the top of my head with a loud crack. My arms dropped and my knees buckled. I was stunned to immobility. Then the second one landed. This one put me out, dropped me to the floor, forced the involuntary release of my bowels. That's how hard he hit me.

I was only out for a matter of seconds, but when I came to on the floor of the bar, bloody, eyes swollen almost shut, befouled and hurting, some little frat boy was astraddle of me, cursing and cuffing me. I struggled against him, broke loose, got to my feet. I was completely sober now and scared to death.

"I quit." I held my hands up to the little frat boy, the pack of the others around him, facing me. "You win."

"Go to hell." The little guy snarled and shoved me hard in the chest. I stumbled back across the bar, reeling, crashing into the jukebox.

I held up my hands again in surrender. Somehow that stopped them for the moment, or something did. I looked around for an avenue of escape. To my immediate left was a short hallway leading to the bar's kitchen, which was on the right side of the hallway. Straight through was the back door, a way out. While I stood there, indecisive, trembling, confused, filthy, the cook came bustling out toward me.

"C'mon, man. Get out of here. These people are tryin' to kill you."

He motioned to me and I went, down the hallway, to the back door he held open, and out of the bar to safety. I don't remember if I thanked him, I hope I did. Outside the bar in the cold air, I ran. I ran as fast as I could back to the house, losing a heel off one of the service brogans I wore. Running in terror, the full import of the fight began to sink in. I was lucky these guys hadn't really, seriously hurt me.

Back at the house, I threw off my clothes, climbed into the downstairs shower and let the hot water cleanse me, felt it stinging my battered face, washing off the filth, the blood, the shame, the remaining fear. I was drying myself off, feeling my almost closed eyes and swollen lip, the gash on the back crown of my head from the bartender's blackjack, when my friends burst in.

Ruthie almost cried when she saw me. Billy and Russell helped me get dressed. Walt came out to see what was up and he drove us all to the student infirmary, not once saying "I told you so."

I spent a painful, sleepless night in the infirmary, my head wrapped like a mummy from the concussion I'd received, my scalp stitched up (only four were required), my face, mouth and teeth numb. Next morning I went home. Sometime Sunday, the local cops dropped by to see if I wanted to press charges, but that seemed foolish so I declined.

Remarkably, by the time we went back to school on Monday, my battered face was practically back to normal with a little swelling left and some discoloration remaining around the eyes and mouth. The outside of me healed remarkably quickly. It took a while longer for the inside to do the same.

My Family Did a Better Job of Trying to Take Me Out Than Those Frat Boys Did

YOU THINK THOSE punks in the bar kicked my fanny? Well, my own family had done a lot better than that, and they'd done it when I was only a kid.

The first attempt on my life has already been described. That was when my oldest brother's sharp little pocket knife slipped and he thought he cut my guts out. That was kill the baby number one.

As you may recall, of course, the little knife hadn't even scraped the skin on my scrawny little stomach. It was good enough, however, for a big screaming, crying episode and an opportunity for me and my siblings to go completely nutso. We were squealing and hollering and howling over my imminent demise. Unfortunately, at least for the nefarious plans of my siblings, that initial plan failed, went astray, came up short so to speak.

Before the "knifing," they had also tried to drown me in a tub. Oh, yeah, they admit to it. They were supposed to be taking care of me while our mother did something else. Sure they were. Apparently the first thing I did was fall in the tub and bang the side of my head on the edge. I still have a small scar beside my left eye, I think it's my left eye, to testify to the murderous intent of my brothers and sister.

Apparently the fall in the tub produced a similar "nutso" experience for my loving siblings because, as they tell it, there was considerable squawking and consternation about what to do with the stupid little baby who had crashed down into the tub and would no doubt be drowning any minute now and what the heck are we gonna tell mom when she gets back and the little ding dong is dead?

Amazingly, I survived this rash attempt on my life as well. The next try was by my mother. A remarkable event since when I was only a tiny baby she and my Aunt Helen had brought me back, seriously, from nearly dying. In that case, motherly, maternal instinct won out and those two incredibly brave and sweet ladies dipped the end of a little handkerchief into some whiskey and applied same spirit to my little mouth and tongue when I was all but finished breathing.

Glorious women that they were, they coaxed my little system back to life. I probably never thanked them enough, or even at all, for saving my life. I didn't learn about this until I was grown, but I'm sure after they saw my development over the years they probably shook their heads in wonder over why such kindness would be repaid with such a reprobate son and nephew!

Nonetheless, the next assault on my life occurred in the presence of my mother who, though not actively responsible for what happened to me, was sitting right there beside me. We were somewhere, someone's house I suppose, and I was sitting on a stool of some kind drinking hot chocolate from a cup and holding my little teddy bear in my little arms. Like the dingleberry that I was and am, I leaned too far back on the stool and, whoops, came crashing down backward. I hit the floor hard on my back, but the worst part was that I hit the back of my head on the baseboard. Ouch.

Once again, I wasn't hurt quite as badly as all my caterwauling would lead someone to expect, but I was bleeding from a cut on the back of my head. The doctor sewed the cut up with a few stitches and I was none the worse for wear, except for a scar that is clearly visible back there on my head should anyone go digging around in what remains of my hair to check the validity of this story.

The incident led to my teddy bear getting a permanent name, Cocoa, and he stayed in the family all the way through my first niece, Mary Ellen, who kept the poor little bear until his eyes and buttons and arms and everything else finally fell off and rotted away. She couldn't bear to part with Cocoa, and he was a bond between us that still lasts today.

Next attempt on my life, back to my oldest brother. This time he tried to take me out in a car. He had some kind of little coupe I think it was, sort of like a miniature tank as I recall, and we were zooming along a dirt road in the country. I was so small still that I was standing in the seat beside my insanely driving brother. This guy's belief at the time was that there was no rate of speed, no matter how high, that he could not safely maneuver whatever beat up car he was driving around whatever corner might be coming up. Forty-five degree corner on slick asphalt, no problem, sixty-degree corner in the rain, ditto, ninety-degree dirt road in the country at fifty miles an hour, easy money.

Unfortunately for the two of us that day, my brother's philosophy failed him, or the laws of physics, or something did. The bottom line was that we didn't make the corner. We shot across the road, banged over a ditch, and shot out into a field. The brakes worked well enough to stop us out in the field. Neither one of us was hurt, not one little bit. But I take this as an attempt on my life regardless and held a healthy fifty plus year grudge against my brother for it.

The last attempt on my life was not so much life-threatening as it was stomach-turning. Here's what happened. When I was about nine or so somebody gave me a little corncob pipe, as a joke present I guess. Well, I took it seriously and soon took to finding the butts of my mother's Lucky Strike cigarettes, unrolling the little bit of paper on them and dumping the remaining tobacco into my pipe. I did this when no one was around, of course, but I was puffing away regularly.

My oldest brother (see a pattern here, yet?) and my sister decided (or were perhaps egged on by my mom who probably wasn't keen on her nine year old firing up tobacco) that they should cure me of this offensive habit. What they did, unbeknownst to me, was buy a cigar and load it with anything they could stuff into it. I think they jammed horse hair, grass (the lawn kind, not the good kind), tiny pieces of sticks, whatever they could find into the cigar, and then they gave it to me to smoke all by myself.

I was thrilled to get to openly smoke this big old cigar. I thought I was cool. We hopped into my brother's car (once again, the "driver") and with them in the front seat and me in the back, we took a drive around town. I was enjoying that cigar, too, up until about ten minutes after we took off. We turned onto Arkansas Avenue from Maple Street over by the university when I began to feel a little funny. It started with a little nausea. Then I got a headache. Then I got sick.

"Something wrong, squirt?" My sister noticed me getting sick. My brother checked me out in the rearview mirror.

"You okay?"

"I don't feel so good." I noticed they were smiling instead of sympathizing with my plight.

"How's that cigar, so far?"

"Oh." I moaned.

"What's wrong?" My sister acted like she didn't know.

"Ugh."

We drove about another half block and I was really sick by then.

"I gotta stop." I sort of whispered, gagging. I was getting ready to throw up.

"Thought you were enjoying that cigar." Big brother tormented me.

"I'm gonna puke." I warned him.

"He looks green." My sister observed.

"He'll be all right."

"Agh." I belched. "Stop. Pull over. I'm gonna throw up."

I guess they finally got the message. My brother pulled over to the curb, me rolling down the window as he did. I stuck my head out and let fly. I hurled big time. It felt terrible and my head spun. I almost passed out. After another episode out the window, I leaned back against the back seat of the car and sighed deeply.

"You done with that cigar?" My brother wanted to know.

"God yes." I tossed the darned thing right out the window.

That was the last time I smoked anything for several years. I would smoke a stray cigarette or little cigar here and there with my buddies as I grew up but I never had the urge to smoke until I went into the service. My family had taught me a lesson. Too bad I didn't learn it well enough to never have smoked again. What the heck, they gave it their best shot. After all, what are brothers and sisters for except for tormenting and making little brothers miserable? I mean, after all.

Writer, Writer—
Too Much Enthusiasm
for So Little Encouragement

A FEW MONTHS AFTER those fraternity bums kicked my butt in that bar in Warrensburg, I took my first and only, could you guess, creative writing class. It was the spring of 1970, perhaps the happiest and most memorable few months of my life, certainly up to that point anyway.

My creative writing teacher was a guy named Harry and the class liked him a lot. He had a positive attitude and tried to help us neophytes in the development of whatever writing skills we might or might not have. Harry was a little wild, given to enjoying his life as a college teacher in the 1960s atmosphere that still permeated campuses even after the decade changed and for several more years afterward—as many of you may remember.

We, his students, could tell that Harry partied a lot and we assumed he was smoking a lot of weed and drinking a lot of wine. We also knew that he was carrying on with one of the girls in the class, but nobody gave a darn. We thought it was funny and invented bizarre sexual scenarios after the girl showed up in class with bruises all over the back sides of her knees. Easy, Harry, easy boy.

Unfortunately, at some point in the semester, Harry came unglued. One day we went to class but he wasn't there. A representative of the college informed us that he was ill and would return as soon as possible. We soon learned that Harry had had a small breakdown of some kind and needed to take some time off from the rigors of teaching.

The school, as they should have, tried to find us a suitable substitute, but this was the 60s, in spirit if not in actual fact, and as a group we flatly rejected the substitute. We wanted Harry and only Harry to instruct us in the arcane rituals of creative writing. When the school insisted that we return to class, we boycotted. And we won for crying out loud. It was remarkable. None of us went back to class until poor old Harry, bedraggled and rather subdued, returned to teach us. We were happy to see him back.

Now before Harry temporarily vanished, an incident occurred in class that forever changed my life. Harry had us trying our hands at poetry to begin with and we would read our poor little attempts to the class for their and Harry's evaluation. As I mentioned, Harry was more into trying to help us feel like we were writers than in showing us how that might happen.

One day I read a newly created poem of mine in class. It was called "Alka Seltzer Morning," or something like that, and it was this poem (a considerably revised version under the title "Feeling Gray" was published some 40 years later), or more accurately Harry's reaction to it, that had such an impact on me. Before I go on about this, I need to lay a little groundwork, give a little background on how easily I am moved to take up powerful dreams.

It all started the first year I ever played baseball back when I was a kid. I was a small ten year old when I tried out for Little League. Because I had not played much ball and was so little, they put me in the City Park League. It was for kids who weren't good or who hadn't played before. Well, I was enthusiastic and in love with baseball so I quickly caught onto the game. By late in our short season I was playing well.

In our final game, the coach brought me in in the middle innings

J. B. Hogan and friends, back row (left to right), Marv Glendening, Donna Hamann, Thomas Altvater, Walt Gum; front row (left to right), J. B. Hogan, Steve Perkins, Warrensburg, MO, Spring 1970.
J. B. Hogan Collection

to pitch (my throwing arm was not strong but I was accurate). Luck would have it that I managed to hold the other team down and then I drove in what would be the winning runs as well. We were the home team and ahead, so I had to pitch the last inning and I got the other team out for the win. My teammates mobbed me on the final out, cheering and yelling, and they lifted me up on their shoulders and carried me off the field.

Do you know what something like that does to a little guy with almost no self-confidence and with zero experience of this type? Well, what it did for me was put in a dream of playing baseball that stuck with me until I was almost twenty-five years old, way past any chance I ever had (and I really never had one) of playing pro ball. In short, it ruined me.

On the positive side, it did give me a dream to strive for. A goal. A hope. Something to try to achieve in life. I've known a lot of people in my life, who never had any kind of dream for their lives, not even a silly, unattainable one like wanting to be a major league baseball player. I feel sorry for those people really.

Okay, so what was the point of that digression? The point was that the same thing happened when it came to imagining myself as a writer. When I wrote that little poem for Harry's creative writing class, his simple reaction to it engendered in me my next big dream, to be a writer. It was the second big dream of my life and the one that has stuck with me.

What was this earth-shattering statement that Harry made, one that was the equivalent of being carried off the playing field by your teammates and that altered how I have thought about myself since that spring of 1970? When I finished my little poem I waited for a reaction, hoping it would be positive. Harry paused for a moment, then smiled and said with considerable enthusiasm, "Now that was a real poem."

And that was all it took. I was done for. I had the writing disease. From that moment forward I thought of myself as a writer and that is all I have ever wanted to be since that fine spring day so long ago.

You might think, given my lack of success at writing over the next two to three decades that I would curse Harry for saying such a thing, lo, these nearly forty years hence. But I don't. I thank him and I appreciate what he did, even if he was only trying to be positive and didn't even think the poem was all that good.

Not succeeding to the level you hope for in attaining your life's goal can surely be depressing and frustrating, as I know very well indeed, but to not have a dream, to have never had a dream, now that's truly sad.

That's the kind of failure that I couldn't bear to have experienced in my own life. I may not be a big, successful writer, but I have done all right in the last several years. And more importantly, I did have a dream, always, and because an upbeat teacher in a small school in the middle of nowhere Missouri liked one poem I wrote. That's cool, if you ask me. A darn lucky break.

Tin Soldiers
and Nixon Coming

NEWS OF THE shootings at Kent State on May 4, 1970 ran through the campuses of the United States like a prairie fire, which in a sense it was. It is difficult now, these many years hence, to express the intensity of emotions felt. Particularly among young people, and most especially among those who considered themselves part of the "movement" already strongly opposed to the policies of the "establishment."

Outrage and anger exploded nearly everywhere and schools were either disrupted or shutdown altogether. At CMS we held services for the dead on Thursday, as I recall, and on Friday planned a big demonstration.

I still remember that demonstration vividly. We gathered at our house on Market Street, we always just called it 209, and then went up by school to join the main body of protesters. As the group of maybe five hundred people wound its way through the streets of Warrensburg, a large number for our conservative little school, there were repeated chants and cheers expressing our displeasure not only with the shootings of fellow students in Ohio but also for the reason campuses had been most recently radicalized, Nixon's illegal incursions into and bombing of Laos and Cambodia.

About halfway through the walk a cool thing happened. We were marching down a residential street in the 'Burg on our way to a large park where we would gather for speeches and so forth and as we walked along hollering out our slogans and so forth, we passed a little house with a man and woman in the front yard.

Given the circumstances and the time and place, most of us figured they might yell or boo at us. To our surprise, however, while the woman remained where she was standing by the house, the man suddenly broke from the yard and with a wave and a cry ran out into the street to join us. When he did that we, almost all of us to the man and woman, let loose this shout of support and joy.

The man's act of joining us might have been the most impulsive, overt, and communal act of dissidence he had done or would ever do in his life.

THE STUDENT receives 5 awards for excellence

THE STUDENT staff won five of the seven major "Best in State" awards for excellence in writing in individual class A competition at the Missouri Collegiate Newspaper contest at the University of Missouri School of Journalism last Friday.

In addition to this the staff won 21 number 1 (Excellent) ratings, and seven number 11 (Superior) ratings.

Best in State awards went to Dave Brittain for both Feature story and Editorial; Diane O'Brien for Critical Review; Jerry Hogan for Sports story; and Patrick Stark for Art-Cartoon.

Outstanding number 1 ratings were earned by David Brittain for two Feature stories , two Editorials, Special Column, and News story; Jenny Ailor for In-Depth story, two Feature stories, and a News Story; Jerry Hogan for Sports feature, News Story and In-Depth story; Patrick Stark for three Art-Cartoons; Joyce Ruark for a Critical Review; J. W. Rudzik for two

Special Columns; Debra Stobaugh for an Editorial; and Diane O'Brien for a Critical Review.

Superior (number II) ratings were earned by Mark McGuire for a sports story and a Special Column; Paulette Reistad for a sports feature; Sheldon Jones for Photography; Cynthia Schwalm for an In-depth story; Mary Cooper for an Editorial; and Larry Clifton for Advertisement.

In the past two years THE STUDENT has won two First Place Awards from Scholastic Press Association, Columbia University; nine major "Best in State" awards, 32 Excellent writing awards, and 12 Superior writing awards.

Other schools in class A are the University of Missouri at Columbia, University of Missouri at Kansas City, University of Missouri at St. Louis, Washington University, and Southeast Missouri State College.

Phil Carter, assistant professor of journalism, advises the newspaper staff.

THE STUDENT is the official campus publication of Central Missouri State College and is published weekly, September through August, except for examination periods and holidays. Entered as second class matter at the Post Office in Warrensburg, Missouri, Zip Code 64093 under the act of March 3, 1879.   Subscription rate: $3.00
Missouri College Newspaper Association Outstanding Newspaper Award 1956, 1968
Columbia Scholastic Press Association First Place, 1969-70.

Adviser	Mr. Phil Carter
Editor	David Brittain
Managing Editor	Debra Stobaugh
News Editor	Mary Cooper
Assistant to the News Editor	Cynthia Schwalm
Feature Editor	Jennifer Ailor
Sports Editor	Mark McGuire
Assistant to the Sports Editor	Sheldon Jones
Literary Editor	Jerry Hogan
Photographer	Stan Bohon
Business Manager	Gary Lakey

J. B. Hogan awards and position, The Student, *Central Missouri State University (now University of Central Missouri), May 1971.*
J. B. Hogan Collection

It was a special moment and all of us reveled in the excitement of it. Little moments like that, we thought in those days, might lead to the real revolution, the one that would change America into a finer and better place.

At the big park, we gathered in a large semi-circle, the group I was with hanging together in a flat area out and to the left of the make-shift stage upon which mostly student leaders held forth on the vileness of the Kent State shootings and the illegal acts in Southeast Asia.

Sometime in the middle of the demo, a comical episode occurred. There was a guy on campus named Leroy who was known as the most rabid acidhead around. He was a completely mellow, likeable guy who was always tripping. He ran a little place in downtown Warrensburg where people read their poetry and others came to play their guitars and sing, a classic coffee shop.

Given that he was popular, and generous as could be with his acid, Leroy was always surrounded by people, especially girls. It was almost like he had his own entourage.

On the day of our Kent State demonstration, Leroy was nowhere to be seen at first. He hadn't been at the forming up point and no one had seen him join the group as it progressed toward the park. About midway through the speechifying, though, Leroy made his entrance, and quite an entrance it was, too.

The first indication of his arrival was a kind of low stirring of sound on the opposite side of the demonstration where there was a small rise in the park. We turned to see what the mild commotion was about and then spotted Leroy coming along the little hill, his group of babes in tow. Two of his lovelies were holding onto him, one on each arm, as if he were about to fall down or fly away or both, which he probably was.

Smiling hugely, insanely, foolishly, happily, and like the zen clown that he was, Leroy made his grand entrance to a swelling of laughter and cheers. Everybody liked this guy and although the day was meant to be serious, Leroy's presence lightened the heavy mood in the park for a moment and reminded us that despite the concerted effort of the outside world to clamp down on our spirits, to trample our souls beneath the weight of its hatred and violence, that we could still be free, and wild, and happy.

I have no idea whatever happened to Leroy. I hope he didn't become a statistic in some drug counselor's report somewhere. There were a lot of Leroys back in those days. They were the counterpoint to those of us who got too serious about everything. They were important parts of the would-be revolution, too. Providing, as it were, in the middle of the all too serious confrontation and debate , a spark of the mad, the divine. God rest them all, the Leroys of the world, all gone now these forty years past. Lost forever in history.

Sometimes Things Just Aren't All That Funny

SPRING 1971. MY senior year at CMS and I get some notoriety for winning several journalism awards at the University of Missouri, in competition against other state schools of our size. The same deans about whom I've been reporting in our student newspaper and satirically lambasting in the student government newsletter had to present to me, the only long hair on the newspaper staff, these awards. Point one. Now they know who I am, and they don't particularly like it or me.

Oh, and one story I wrote involving our college president, a simple news story I swear, caused the president to threaten to shut down the school paper. Our advisor, Mr. Carter, to his everlasting credit, refused this fine offer of censorship. He even managed to keep his job somehow.

Fall 1971. I turned down several entry-level cub reporter jobs around the country to attend grad school at CMS. Mistake. The Dean of Admissions called me in right as school was starting to determine if I intended to keep looking like I did. You know, blue jeans, T-shirt, beard, long hair. When I said I did, we began to jaw a little at each other and the next thing I know I'm stomping out of the office after telling him he'd be hearing from my lawyer.

Naturally I didn't have a lawyer, but I'd heard it on TV or somewhere and so I thought it sounded tough. What I was threatening him for was that he'd informed me I could not attend CMS grad school unless I changed my appearance. To be technical, he responded in the affirmative to my question asking if he was saying I could not go to grad school unless I cut my hair and cleaned up.

So all of a sudden I'm not in school. I was living in an upstairs apartment in Knob Noster, a tiny little Air Force town about ten miles from Warrensburg. By this time, one of my 209 buddies, Perk, and his new girlfriend lived below in one apartment and two girls lived across from them in another.

What I'm doing as a ne'er do well non-student is writing a bizarre absurdist play called *To Do or Die* in which all of the characters speak only in clichés. I finished the play and my friend Perk filmed part of it using our student friends as actors but nothing ever came of it, although it was a blast just doing what of it that we did.

I'm also reading Kerouac's Mexico City Blues at this time and I learn from Jacky Kerwacky how to end poems and stories, with a bang, a blast, a strong parting shot. No drifting off, no whimpers. It was an excellent lesson.

Midway through the fall quarter, CMS had an odd quarter system in which you earned semester hours, I got an unexpected letter from school. I'm flunking all my graduate school classes. Hello. I'm not in grad school, remember. I may be a weenie but I'm not taking this crap.

I marched back up to Mr. Dean of Admissions and demanded to know why I'm getting Fs in all the classes he said I couldn't attend. Ey, why? Mr. Dean got nervous and before I left his office he's giving me some song and dance about a "computer error." That's kind of early for that defense, ahead of his time, don't you think? Gotta give the guy credit for that one. Baloney as it was.

Next day or so, I'm in the union, it's a Monday, I'm pretty sure of that. I used to go in and sit in the union while I'm writing the play or reading Kerouac, when somebody pointed out an ACLU guy who is

160   J.B. HOGAN

Hogan Charges Are Dismissed In Court Here

Charges against Jerry Bruce Hogan, 26, Knob Noster, were dismissed yesterday afternoon following a preliminary hearing in the Magistrate Court of Judge Roy A. Jones.

Police had alleged Hogan struck a Warrensburg policeman with a rock as officers moved down Anderson Street beside the men's dormitories during an encounter between students and city and college police the night of Oct. 28.

Hogan was arrested in the CMSC Union around noon the next day and charged with felonious assault.

Police had said Hogan was not arrested at the scene because officers were unable to apprehend him at the time, but that positive identification had been made by two Warrensburg policemen.

Hogan, on the other hand, maintained he was not even in Warrensburg at the time, but at home in Knob Noster.

During yesterday's preliminary hearing four persons testified that Hogan had been at an apartment at 400 West McPherson Street in Knob Noster at the time of the disturbance Oct. 28.

Arrest clipping, Warrensburg Daily Star-Journal, *Warrensburg, Missouri, Fall 1971.*
J. B. Hogan Collection

on campus to help somebody out with a case against the school. In those days, CMS was big on getting after students and would take cases all the way to the United States Supreme Court before giving up. Man, they ran a tight ship.

I walked up to the ACLU guy and introduced myself. He's not interested in taking my case but he gave me some advice. Write a letter. Make the school put down in writing why you weren't allowed into grad school. Let me know how that goes and we'll see about your case.

I sent the letter the next day, Tuesday. Thursday night there's a panty raid (can you believe that with all the political stuff going on in those days?) in Warrensburg. At this time, as I mentioned before, I lived in Knob Noster, ten miles away, and I am not in the 'Burg or even close to it. But the next day, Friday morning, my life came apart at the seams.

I went to the union. I'm sitting at a table by myself. I'm

writing my play. I look up and see this weird older guy who always sits way back in back of the union checking out all us long hairs at our tables. I go back to writing, suddenly my table is surrounded. It's two city cops and a campus one.

"You Jerry Hogan?"

"Yes?"

"You're under arrest."

"Under arrest? What for?"

"Come with us."

They stood me up and because I was hauled in so many times in the service I know the drill. I put my arms behind my back in the parade rest position and calmly walked out with the cops. They took me into a small room off the main hallway of the union and read me my rights. The charge, felonious assault of a police officer. Later I found out that carried a maximum penalty of three to five years in the Missouri State Penitentiary. Ouch.

"I didn't do it."

"Let's go."

They handcuffed me and led me back out into the big hallway. Remarkably, it's when classes were changing, the union filling with students. Curious kids are watching the proceedings. They look worried, interested, amused. I try to act like it's no big deal, only me getting busted and being hauled off by the cops.

Luckily, we made it down the hallway and outside with only a few more swear words and insults being hurled at the police. In retrospect, I see how cool it was to be hauled off publicly like that, but at the time I wanted everyone to take it easy. I was the one going to jail.

The ride to the police station was uneventful. The cops said nothing about the insults, all they did was a weak version of good cop/bad cop.

"The only thing I'm going to say," hey, I'd been in custody probably at least ten times in the service, I knew how the routine went, "is that I didn't do it. That's it."

I had managed to stop smoking for six months when I got arrested. As we walked into the police station, the jail was in the same building to the back and side of the main desk, I bummed a cigarette off one of the arresting officers, the good cop. I was immediately hooked again on nicotine.

The resolution to all this was positive for me, a new lawyer looking to make a name for himself in the local community took my case and requested that my preliminary hearing be held like a trial. The courtroom was absolutely jam-packed with the interested and curious. It was an intense and, at least for me, memorable day.

To get to this point, of course, I first had to be sprung from jail. My bond had been set at one thousand dollars, a high amount in those days and twice that of anyone else arrested during the "panty raid." My friends came up with the money and hustled to find a bondsman to get me out. Thanks to them, I only had to stay in the city/county jail for about four hours. They were lucky to get me out at all. The sheriff was going fishing that afternoon and they barely got the bail money to him in time to secure my release before he left for the weekend.

Over the next week or so, different groups, like the campus Vets organization, donated money to my defense fund and there was even a fair-sized rally held at which Perk spoke on my behalf and more money was raised. Not just for me but also for a girl who had gotten on CMS' bad legal side by trying to live off campus. CMS had the old "in loco parentis" philosophy and girls in particular were corralled tightly.

When the preliminary hearing rolled around only a few days after my arrest and release, my lawyer asked for as many long hairs to be there as we could muster. He wanted, among other things, to show that the police might have mistaken my identity.

During the course of the hearing, which lasted most of the day, my lawyer called about six or seven witnesses on my behalf. The prosecution argued that I had hit a city cop with a rock during the "panty raid." The first thing my lawyer did to weaken their case was get them to admit that it wasn't even a rock that had been thrown at them but an apple core. That caused a lot of laughter in the courtroom.

In retrospect, the key elements of the day that worked the most in my behalf were having so many witnesses on my side, and the fact that I, because I was completely innocent of the charges, could take the stand in my own behalf.

If you are ever in a situation like this, I recommend you take the stand. Do not be afraid. If you didn't do what you are charged with, nothing in the world can beat your own testimony to that point. Don't let the system frighten or confuse you. Stick to your guns. Fight 'em tooth and nail.

The final disposition of the case, when all the arguments were over, was sometime around three or four in the afternoon, I think it was. I heard the little old judge say the best and probably most important words of my life, up to that point anyway. I was in a sort of fever of fear, anticipation, and dread, almost afraid to watch or listen. But I did. Ah, I still hear the words across these many years.

"Mister Prosecutor." The judge set a sheaf of papers on the desk before him. Sweat was no doubt pouring down my brow and back at this point. "You couldn't convict this man in any court in the state of Missouri. Charges are dismissed for lack of evidence."

There was a pause while the portent of the judge's words sank in to me and to the big crowd of onlookers. Then there was a big burst of applause that lasted a good spell, until we heard the sounds of people rising, shuffling, preparing to leave the courtroom.

As for me, I had heard the judge's words but it took a few seconds for them to register properly in my brain. My lawyer clapped me on the back and shook my hand and then all of the tension drained out of my system like a dam breaking. I sighed deeply and slid down in my seat.

"Oh, my." I might have said. I'm sure it was nothing momentous.

Leaving the courtroom, I was swamped by well-wishers, people congratulating me on beating "the system." All I knew was that I wasn't going to have to do time for something I didn't do. Some people told me, "See, the system works."

I had trouble with that for a long time. I felt that if the system had been working, somebody would not have decided unilaterally and falsely that I had been involved in this incident in the first place. Who had identified me? Why? When? Where? Those were questions unanswered then, and still unanswered today.

Of course, it doesn't matter at all now. Not anymore. Too many years have passed. And it was too small a case, in too small a town. A blip in time. Nothing more. On a personal level, naturally, it was more than that to me. I couldn't work around town. My name had been on the front page of the Warrensburg paper and people don't like to hire you after things like that.

I left town not long after and went to Columbia where I stayed with friends who'd moved there earlier. I worked for a while as a delivery man's helper on a dry cleaning van servicing restaurants all around town. It was an okay job but not exactly like being a cub reporter or getting my Master's degree.

I only stayed in Columbia a couple of months before I moved on. One funny note about that time, not necessarily funny ha ha, but sort of. While I was in Columbia, I tried to keep a low profile. During my first week in town, however, I went up to the University of Missouri to hang out at their union. Inside on a big table I see the student newspaper, The Maneater. I pick it up to check it out. So, what do I see? You guessed it, a story about CMS which included the details of my arrest.

Yikes, my cover was most likely blown. I shortly found out that the local Columbia newspaper covered my arrest as well. It didn't matter much for the time being anyway. My job at the dry cleaning company played out and I left Columbia sometime toward the end of 1971. I would have to take my personal show on the road again, and that's what I did, after a brief respite with my friends back in the 'Burg and Knob Noster.

Hitching to Boulder in February Is Not the Smartest Thing to Do

B Y FEBRUARY 1972, I was finished in Warrensburg, Columbia, and most any places in between. I was out of school, out of work and out of prospects. The perfect time to take a road trip, right? Well, that's exactly what me and my friend Russell did.

———————————

Early February, Twenty Above

Twenty above, standing by the Higginsville exit, two onion and cheese sandwiches apiece and five dollars between us. A friend's VW disappearing down Highway 13 like the last link to safety and comfort, which it was.

It was cold on the highway but we only had to wait a little over an hour for the first ride. It was a perfume salesman. His car was soft and warm inside and had a strong feminine odor. He talked about his job, how he traveled, some of the fascinating people he met, how young people were okay by him.

But he only went to Kansas City and dropped us off on I-70 right before the road turned north to head up to St. Joseph. We reluctantly went back into the cold, the buildings of downtown looming up in the background, gray, impersonal, unconcerned. The perfume salesman gave each of us a bottle of cheap cologne and we stowed them in our bags wishing it had been something warm to eat or drink. It was still morning.

"Hey, white boys." The girl called. "Hey, you need a ride?"

We hustled down the embankment to the waiting car, a long, white Pontiac. There were three girls, two skinny and one fat, and one guy, a totally nodded out doper. They were going to Denver.

At any speed the car weaved and floated from side to side, scaring the heck out of us. As soon as they crossed the state line into Kansas one of the tall skinny girls took the wheel, put the Pontiac at about 100 mph and left it there.

The car sailed, literally sailed, down the interstate and the girls started telling about shooting smack and began harassing the stoned out dude. They were kind of bitchy girls and one time they put a match into the guy's face and burned some of his beard. It smelled awful but didn't seem to bother him. He was definitely gone.

Somewhere past Lawrence they stopped for gas and the girl driving decided it would be a good idea to pull out right away without paying. Take off without removing the gas hose from the tank. At the last minute she changed her mind and paid the bill. At that point, we were convinced that weaving back and forth down the interstate at 100 miles an hour wasn't so bad after all. At least there wouldn't be cops after us, too. It was a relative sort of thing.

An hour or so later, the skinny girl driver suddenly pulled over onto the shoulder of the road and announced that they were turning back for Kansas City. Russell and I were presently in the absolute middle of nowhere.

"This is it." The driver girl looked at us.

"We gotta go back." The other skinny girl explained.

"Yeah, we have to." The dude mumbled.

"Shut up." The fat girl hit him on the arm. He just stared off into space.

Russell Gerling (left) and J. B. Hogan, Warrensburg, Missouri, Late Spring, 1970.
Photo by Thomas Altvater

We climbed out. It was the warmest part of the day. It still felt cold as hell.

"They won't be goin' back to Kansas City."

"No?" I watched the Pontiac fade into the distant horizon.

"They dumped us 'cause we didn't have dope."

"Think so?"

"Yeah, the main driver girl was mad about that. I heard her say it at the station back there."

"We're probably better off." I surmised.

"I suppose. But this sure ain't nowhere."

"No."

"This is Kansas."

"Exactly."

"They probably thought we were bigots, too."

"Let's eat one of the sandwiches."

"Good idea."

A Nice Farm Girl

She was a nice farm girl and she took us all the way to Hays. By then it was getting late and the temperature was dropping faster than our spirits.

"You boys know how to read?" The highway patrolman was gruff with us. He was about ready to kick our cans into storage for a few days, but we didn't give him any grief and we were clean. At least our Federal and Kansas records, that is.

"You can't stand up here on the highway. You'll have to wait off the highway by the entrance ramp. Before it. You can't be a traffic hazard. Clear?"

Clear. We walked down to the bottom of the ramp and waited. It was beginning to get real cold. The sun was almost gone.

Another hitchhiker hung with us for a while. He said somebody had taken a shot at him somewhere this side of St. Louis. Probably didn't like people bummin' rides, he suggested. Sometimes he went to airports and hitched rides on private planes. We weren't exactly sure about that one. Then the sun went down. We started pacing. Back and forth. Back and forth. It was dark. It was cold.

This Girl Was Young

This girl was young and drove a yellow Plymouth. At first we were so warm we fell asleep in the car. Later we shared the driving but finally had to stop and let everyone sleep for a while.

We reached the outskirts of Denver while it was still dark but beginning to lighten up. On the way to Boulder, the girl let us know she was sixteen, from San Diego, and that she had stolen the Plymouth from her dad and taken off. We looked at each other and shook our heads.

When we got to Boulder it was gray. Light, but no sun yet. The mountains drove up into the sky beyond the town and hung there, dominant, oppressive.

"I'm going on to California maybe later today or tomorrow. If you guys want to go on with me, let's meet up at the CU union or be around there and I'll look for you. I got people here. I want to visit them."

"Us, too. Maybe we'll see you later."

"You serious," I asked Russell when the girl was gone, "go on to California? I thought this was where we were going."

"You're right."

"Forget California."

"Yeah, forget it. There's millions of people out here. We can find a place to crash."

"All right, then, we made it."

"Let's get somethin' to eat." Russell pointed to a diner up the street.

"I'm for that."

"Later we look for something to do."

"And a place to crash."

"Right on."

We walked into the small, early-hours diner and ordered eggs, potatoes, toast, and hot chocolate. Outside you could feel the presence of the mountains, cold, powerful, unconcerned. We'd gone as far as we were going. We didn't think about the under-aged girl in her daddy's stolen car, or California. We'd go ahead and give Colorado a run for its money. That's what we had intended to do anyway. We had at least made it to here. That would be enough for the time being.

Tribalism, Ripoffs, and One Dumb Kid Reporter Who Should've Known Better

BOULDER LASTED ONE month for me. I worked one night as a dishwasher in a Mexican food place a block or so from Pearl and Broadway and then got a job as a garbage man. That lasted a couple of weeks, but a contract fell through and since I was last in I was first out. I felt so directionless then that I went back to Missouri, leaving Russell to fend for himself for another few months. I only stayed in Missouri briefly then headed up to Lincoln, Nebraska where I crashed on my mother's couch and got a job as a reporter and assistant editor of an Indian newspaper.

For six weeks then, in the early spring of 1972, I worked for what passed itself off as an Indian newspaper. I did manage to write a few stories and we got at least one issue out during that time but mostly I hung out in Lincoln's Indian Center listening to the young guys, mostly Viet Nam vets, complain about other minorities and other tribes in the Sioux Nation. It was disappointing and disenchanting. They treated me well, all things considered, but it was depressing to see and hear all the internal and external bickering.

In the end, I got ripped off by the white owner/publisher of the paper for six weeks' work. I didn't get a single dime from the guy. And on top of that, I was so stupid that I signed a phone bill in my own name, not realizing I should have signed as a representative of

Nebraska Trails

Official Newspaper
Of The Indian People Of Nebraska

BULK RATE
POSTAGE PAID
LINCOLN, NEBR.
PERMIT 241

Published by Nebraska Indian Information & Publication Center, Inc.
1st Christian Church Bldg.   16th & K Lincoln, Nebraska   P.O. Box 81281   Phone No. 475-6977

Vol.II, No. 1   May 5, 1972   35¢ Per Copy

Published as an official newspaper and
public information project by the Nebraska
Indian Information and Publication Center
Inc. member American Indian Press Organ-
ization. First Christian Church, 16th and K,
Box 81281. Lincoln, Nebraska, 68501.

SUBSCRIPTION: 52 issues for $9.00

Editorial policy in no way reflects the
views of advertisers.

Robert Mackey   - President
Lavoy DaCoteau   - Vice President
Jim Rogers   - Project Director
Jerry Hogan   - Assistant Editor
Rev. Jerry Dunn   - Treasurer
Lee Kills Enemy   - Secretary
Keith Stephenson   - Assistant Secretary

Cover of Indian Trails *newspaper, J. B. Hogan, Assistant Editor, Lincoln, Nebraska, May 1972, J. B. Hogan Collection*

the paper. So I ended up getting stuck with a seventy-five dollar bill. I tried to fight it but a collection agency came after me so I bit the bullet and paid it off over time.

That was my only foray into the world of working journalism, such as it was, despite previous and later offers from papers in Arizona and Florida. With such a crappy track record, it makes perfect sense to me why I never pursued that particular career path. I opted instead to later go back to grad school to get a Masters and a Ph.D.

I would learn to be a writer by reading all the great writers and letting all their greatness work its way into and through me and come out the other side as another, if not great, at least fairly decent writer myself. The jury remains out on that one.

The Mowing Crew Never Cut Down a Full Grown Marijuana Plant

FOR THE TWO and a half remaining years I lived in Lincoln, I worked for the City Parks and Recreation Department. I was on the five-man mowing crew. In the winter we were the designated outdoor crew, the guys scooping snow and ice on sidewalks and lakes around town so that the citizens could see their tax dollars at work. We didn't mind it all that much. We were young and rowdy. It was okay.

The Parks jobs were what I called city welfare employment for freaks. Almost all of us on the mowing crew and on the tree trimming crews were long hairs. You could get these jobs and not have to change who you were, either on the inside or the outside. It was a good deal. Especially during that era.

Now keep in mind that we may have been hippies to the straight world, but we had pride, both in ourselves and in what we did. All three years (or parts thereof) that I worked there in Lincoln it was ranked the number one Parks Department for cities of its size in the United States, the whole country. We may not have looked like people wanted us to, but we were clearly doing something right.

In the winter they used to make us, the designated outdoor crew, go out to certain small ponds that were frozen over, naturally enough in way sub-zero Lincoln weather, and have us walk around on the ponds all day scooping that tiny little layer of ice that forms overnight on top of the frozen water. Oh, yeah. Back and forth. Back and forth. I remember one day in particular when we began our scooping of the lake a little after sunup, it was around fifteen below. That's not comfortable.

In late spring, summer, and early fall we were the mowing crew, going from park to park all around town. We mowed with care, using specific patterns and procedures, and the parks always looked great when we got done with them. In those days, there was a lot of ditch weed around (poor quality plants that were basically volunteers from somebody tossing seeds out in the parks) and we would occasionally see a plant growing.

Even though we knew this weed was worthless, it was both a joke and a point of honor among us not to cut down any large plants with our mowers. If it was a big, tall healthy plant we would mow in a circle around it, leaving it standing all by itself in the middle of the park or by a ditch or outbuilding, wherever it might be. Those were different times and we were only having fun.

One side note—in 1974 I became the lead man on the mowing crew, one of the few pseudo-supervisory positions I've ever held. Two things about it: one, I prided myself on the fact that no one got hurt on my watch; and two, do you remember Charles Starkweather, the guy from Lincoln who went on a killing spree in 1957-1958 with his girlfriend Caril Ann Fugate?

Well, the connection is that while I was lead man, I trained the first woman ever on the mowing crew and her name was Linda Starkweather. She had married Charlie's younger brother. She never knew Charles Starkweather, but she was aware of the notoriety and it's always been one of those odd things to me that I trained her on our crew.

So, back up a bit. One day when we were mowing in the fall of 1973, the regular grass always had one more spurt of growth as the cool weather of autumn set in, I had a major epiphany. I was driving

J. B. Hogan, Spring 1974.
Photo by Carol Jean Perkins

my mower in a park in central Lincoln and suddenly an idea popped into my head. I shut the blade down on my mower and stopped it right in the middle of the park.

"I'm going to be a teacher." I stood up in the saddle of my mower. "I'm going back to graduate school. I'm going to be a teacher."

"What did you say?" One of my crewmates called over to me. He couldn't figure out what was up.

"I'm going to be a teacher. Back to school."

"Back to what?"

"School, back to school."

"Whatever." He turned his mower away and zoomed off to cut the grass in another part of the park.

"Yeah, whatever."

From seemingly out of nowhere, this new idea of my immediate future had exploded into my consciousness. It seemed to make perfect sense. I would go back to school. I would get my masters degree after all and work on becoming a writer. Yes, it made perfect sense. It must have been what I had wanted to do all along. I was absolutely certain of it at that moment.

About a year later, I made my epiphany come true when I returned to graduate school. It wasn't back at CMS, of course, nor even at a logical place like the University of Nebraska. Nope, when I went back to grad school, I went to an institution completely outside the continental United States, a Baby Doc U. some of my friends in later years would joke. But it wasn't a joke of a school at all, it was the University of Puerto Rico in Rio Piedras, Puerto Rico. It was a fine school, at least the English Department part was.

Puerto Rican
Masters

I
T WASN'T LIKE I picked the University of Puerto Rico out of the blue. There were two reasons why I went there. One, I had gone there with friends to visit and had enjoyed that visit so much that the idea of moving to Puerto Rico was not so foreign when I returned to Lincoln.

The second reason I went to UPR was that I had a crappy undergraduate GPA, something like 2.49 overall. CMS was going to let me go to grad school because I had graduated from there but once they tossed me out, going on to an advanced degree became more problematic. UPR, luckily, admitted me on probation and from that time on, with the motivation of an older and more ambitious person, from the beginning of my graduate studies until I completed my Ph.D., I maintained a 4.0 GPA.

UPR, and Puerto Rico in general, was an excellent experience. Mostly great everything—beaches, tropical fruit, new friends, but not so much in super densely populated, crime-ridden San Juan. Overall, however it was a good time. I did well in school. One teacher boosted my ego by telling me I was a "true scholar." And you know me, remember the baseball and the creative writing class stories? One compliment can send me off on a lifetime mission. So that made me a scholar then, in my mind anyway. Because I love school.

At La Finca, professor housing, University of Puerto Rico, early Spring 1976,
J. B. Hogan Collection

I love libraries. I love research. I love writing. What was there to complain about?

And also, I'm surrounded by lovely island women. Beautiful Puerto Rican girls. Oh, my, that's some decent work if you can get it.

Dr. Hogan,
I Presume

I COMPLETED MY M.A. at UPR in sixteen months, including researching and writing my thesis on Philip Roth (I wanted to do one on Hemingway but the existing body of criticism was too daunting for the amount of time I had allotted to get my degree). A few months later I had moved to Tempe, Arizona and begun a three-year program to attain the Ph.D.

At Arizona State University, I made many, many new friends and had a great time. I loved being a student. I loved reading and analyzing literature and I loved the technical stuff, too, learning to translate from the Anglo-Saxon and from Middle English. I was totally committed to the program and I taught all three years as well.

Tempe was a cool place to be then. It's not too bad today, even with the absurd growth of metropolitan Phoenix. They had good, cheap Mexican food places to eat and drink at and there was the Warehouse for submarines and the Chuck Box for hamburgers (although I had stopped eating meat a couple of years before). And there was the Bandersnatch bar where some of us hung out and where I had the only meeting with one of my professors one summer during a guided reading course I took.

I was fired up most of the time at Tempe, what with taking two classes and teaching two each semester, but never ever in all my days was I as excited and energized as I was in the days leading up to my Ph.D. written exams at the end of my second year of Ph.D. studies. I had been preparing for them for almost two years (or many more if you count my undergrad and M.A. days) and I was absolutely wired to take them. This is how they went down.

The exams were given over a ten day span with individual tests based upon your areas of specialization. My four specializations were Modern American Literature (my primary specialty), American Lit. to 1900, Modern British Literature, and Medieval Lit.

I know, I know, what in the world is that Medieval Lit. thing doing there? Well, the truth is, I like the literature of the middle-ages as much as anything else and maybe even more. For one thing, it was a period with everything firmly established. The writing was from so long ago that there was little debate about what was important and what wasn't like there is in the contemporary periods.

So, for the Ph. D. exams, you had to take four three-hour written tests (you were given a fourth hour if you needed it) in the areas you chose. I think the maximum score you could get, was twenty-four, based on making a six on each of the four testing areas. A score of twenty-four, which was a ridiculous High Pass (the best I saw during my time at ASU was my friend Maggie who scored a twenty-two, yee ha). The minimum score to pass was twelve. I believe a score of five on any individual test was considered a High Pass, too, but I can't remember how that worked anymore.

Bottom line, I got fives in Modern American and in Medieval and fours in the other two areas for a solid eighteen. Not a High Pass but a good, solid score. I was pleased. And I had used up all of the available time allotted to me to complete those exams. Oh, yeah, I needed every second of those sixteen hours to get the score I did.

In retrospect, viewing these exams from many years distance, the main thing I remember is how wired I was, how energized I was to take those tests. It was like getting ready for a football game. I mean I

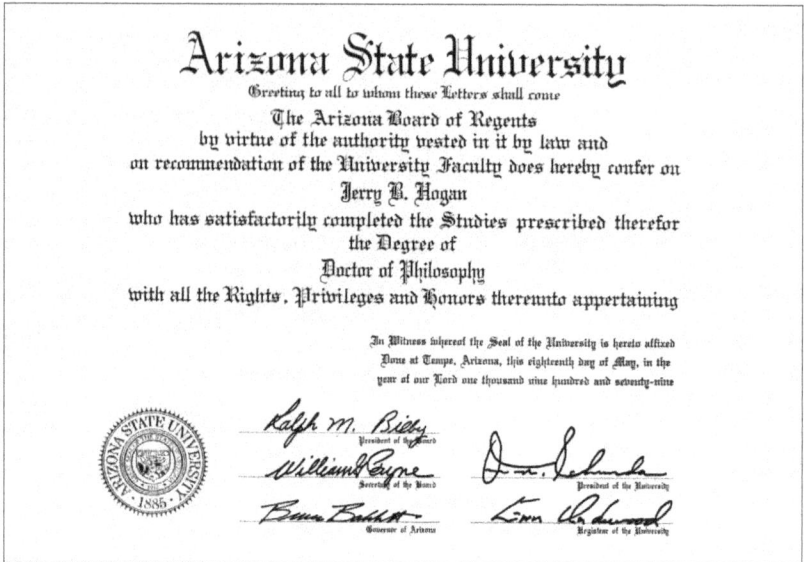

Ph.D. Diploma, Arizona State University, Tempe, Arizona, May 1979

was primed up. In fact, I was so fired up, like on some sort of natural speed if you will, that to this day I have never been the same.

Before the tests, I had the ability to be laid back if I wanted to be. After them, I never came down from the high. It created a kind of psychic energy within me that while it has diminished a fair amount over the years has still left me with a drive for work that never fully subsides. Before those tests, I used to be able to kick back and listen to music or watch TV for hours without feeling any need to get up and do anything. Not after the tests. I always want to be working on something now and that something is usually writing or research related, an extension of exactly what I had to do to prep up for those exams.

Simply put, the Ph.D. written exams changed me forever and I don't mind. Whatever that residual energy is, it gives me the drive to read, write, and research for hours on end without tiring. So that's what I do, most days, even when I don't have to and don't get paid for it. It's who I am now. It's what those tests made of me.

Here's Your Ph. D. Now Go Away

WHEN I COMPLETED the Ph.D., I naturally wanted to get a teaching job. A few people had warned me that jobs were drying up faster than mudholes in the Mojave Desert, but I stormed ahead and got that degree, anyway. I had to do it. I wanted to be a professor for a living while I used summers and other down time to begin my fiction writing career. Things didn't quite work out the way I planned.

First of all, getting a tenure track job in literature at a university at that particular time, I came to realize all too well, was quite difficult. Basically, you had to either have an Ivy League (or near-equivalent) degree, have referees (references) who were well-known figures in your discipline, or already have found a way to publish several top notch academic articles or, better yet, a book. The best case of all, of course, was to do all three. I had none of them.

I also made some decisions that were critical and that, in the end, finished off my academic life before it even got started. For one thing, I turned down a job offer back at UPR. That decision was a career killer. As for the rest of my attempts to secure academic employment, well the competition was simply too strong for me.

The worst case scenario was a tenure track job I applied for at the University of Louisville, I believe it was. Whatever the case, the job was in my special specialty, Modern American Literature. However, the rejection letter indicated that there had been around seven hundred and fifty applications for that one job. 750. I stood no chance whatsoever.

On the positive side, the English Departments at ASU and the University of Arizona in Tucson had, in those days, an exchange program wherein a new Ph.D. from each school would get a one year Visiting Assistant Professor job at the other school. One newbie from ASU to the U of A and vice versa. For the 1979-1980 school year, I managed to get that job at the University of Arizona.

The job turned out to be my one and only year as a full-blown college prof but it was a fine one. The Ooo Aaa (one of the nicknames for the University of Arizona) English Department treated the new exchange Ph.D person (in this case me) well and gave you decent classes to teach.

During the regular school year, over the course of the two semesters I was there, I got to teach three Introduction to Literature classes in addition to the expected composition courses. That was excellent right there and would have made it a good year if nothing else happened.

At the end of spring semester, however, the department needed some people for the first session of summer school and they kept me on to teach classes in American Humor and the American Short Story. Now *that* was outstanding. Summer classes come at you fast and hard, especially in terms of teacher preparation, but I couldn't have gotten better classes if I'd tried. All in all, the UA experience was just fine.

For one thing, I discovered, as I thought I would, that I would have time to seriously begin my fiction writing career as well as teach. Because I taught essentially the same classes in the second semester as I had the first, my preparation time was vastly reduced allowing me the opportunity to begin my first novel in earnest. I had been right about the plan. Teaching would have been the way for me to jump-start and perhaps succeed at a writing career. Unfortunately for me, at the end of the first summer session of 1980 my college teaching career came to an abrupt and final end.

I failed abjectly at landing a job anywhere else (I applied to dozens of colleges and universities, it seemed at the time like it was hundreds). The U of A had two jobs come up during the second semester I was there and I was hopeful of getting one of those but I only made it into the second round because one of the guys on the committee was a young professor who took pity on me. There were over three hundred applicants for the two jobs (334 is the number that I seem to remember).

Of the two people hired, one was an Ivy Leaguer with no teaching experience but with referees whose names I recognized from our textbooks and the other was a guy from California who had already published one critical book and was working on another. Again, I had no chance against people with qualifications like that.

For a long while I was bitter about losing my academic career, and I drifted on an emotional beach of soft and shifting sand. To mix my metaphors, I was a puny little ship, floundering in the rough seas of real life. My only recourse was to tack my pathetic little vessel toward shore. Any shore, anywhere. And that's what I did.

Tucson and Celebrities

U NLIKE THE POST-Ph.D., written exams me, Tucson itself has always had a laid back vibe, especially in comparison to its neighbor to the north Phoenix. Driving can be a bit of a pain but the townsfolk are relatively mellow and there are many places to go hiking in the area—and it has all the stores and restaurants you would expect in a mid-size town. One interesting thing about the place is that, at least back in the day, it had a lot of celebrities in town because they could come in and not be bothered. People noted them but just left them alone. I never saw him in town, but Paul McCartney has, or had, a ranch outside of Tucson for years.

In my time there, I saw several celebrities, big and small, around town. I used to work out at a Nautilus club—so '70s and '80s!—and some famous people used to come there. Besides the local TV stars, probably the biggest name at the club was actor Lee Marvin. I remember working out on a machine and looking right over at Marvin. Everyone just went about their business, no big fuss. He was rumored to be a heavy drinker but I never saw him in any of the bars around town.

Another time, while I was checking out of the club, I stood next to supermodel Cheryl Tiegs for about five minutes while she was speaking to the desk person. I remember thinking that she was pretty all right but that I could see women just as good-looking any time in Tucson. Still, it was an interesting few minutes. It's not like I hang out with supermodels every day!

Sometimes, you might just see a celebrity on a street or shopping. I saw Doug McClure, if you remember him, at a restaurant near the Tucson airport, and from time to time there would be a Linda Ronstadt sighting. She came from an old, highly respected family in town and while I was there two of her brothers, or uncles, were the Police and Fire Chiefs, respectively.

A fun encounter I had once was just outside the University of Arizona on Speedway Boulevard, Tucson's main East-West street. It was in a little grocery called the Spot Market. I was doing some small shopping there when I happened to look up at the next aisle across from me—and I was looking directly at the face of Gene Wilder. Gene Wilder of *The Producers, Bonnie and Clyde,* and *Silver Streak* fame.

We just stared at each other awkwardly for a moment and then went about our business. He knew I recognized him but I just dropped eye contact, pretending it was normal to see Gene Wilder when I went grocery shopping. Still, when I got up to the checkout counter, I did ask the woman he was with if it was for sure him. She laughed and indicated it was him. I think he was in town maybe during the filming of *Stir Crazy.* Anyway, it was a fun encounter and not so uncommon in the Old Pueblo, as Tucson likes to call itself.

International Bland Men & Elephants Outside the Kilaguni Lodge

THAT'S RIGHT, I worked at IBM for several years. In the belly of the corporate beast. A world just about 180 degrees from academia, trust me. But I made many fine friends in there. Friends I've had for the rest of my life or theirs (I've lost several in the last few years).

Other than those people, however, working at and for IBM sucked mostly, as you can imagine. I'm not a corporate kind of guy, never was, never have been, never will be. I thought of it as being back in the service except that I made a lot better money for doing it.

Later I worked for IBM for a lot more years as a contractor. Contracting was much better. I could bail whenever I wanted or needed to and they could dump me out whenever they wanted or needed to. I liked that arrangement. There was no pretense about them taking care of me or managing me, and I was there strictly for the money, no career advancement, no future. Strictly a money arrangement. Basic. Clear. As clean as you can get in the work world.

As Forrest Gump would say, "that's all I have to say about that."

ONE OF THE benefits of working at IBM was that I was making

way more money than I ever had before at any job in my life. Oh, yeah, way more. The result was that I could do some things I had wanted to do for a while and that I had not been able to afford. The first of those was a photo safari to Africa in 1984. Yes, sir, you betcha. Kenya. Animals. Incredible.

It was a two-week trip with the first week starting in Nairobi and looping around the country to the Amboseli and Tsavo West game preserves, then back to Nairobi. The second week was another loop, this one going first to the Samburu preserve up in the northern territory, then swinging back down through Lake Nakuru, and finishing the week with three days and nights on the Masai Mara before returning again to Nairobi.

There's no point in delaying my reaction to this trip. It was terrific. Nothing could detract from the awesome days and nights I spent in Kenya. It was simply extraordinary.

One of the best things that happened was one of the simplest, most basic. My traveling group at Tsavo West stayed at a huge place called the Kilaguni Lodge. Luckily, when we first got there the lodge was almost completely empty (the next day something like one hundred French people arrived). Kilaguni had two large, lighted, red dirt waterholes a hundred yards or so away from the lodge itself. From late in the afternoon throughout the night and into the early morning hours there was a steady stream of animals taking turns drinking at the waterholes.

That alone was thrilling to me but early the next morning, while it was still deeply dark, I had one of the best observational experiences of my life. I had gone to bed around eleven or so, struggling to fall asleep and after tossing and turning finally fell into a fitful slumber. I don't know what woke me up, but I got up quietly, the travel alarm clock showed a few minutes before five a.m., put on a long sleeve shirt and went out onto the balcony of the second-floor room well above the ground. I sat there in silence trying to relax.

It was pleasant on the balcony. The only sounds were coming from animals at or around the waterholes and they were low, natural, and soothing to me. Mount Kilimanjaro was off in the darkness to my left, at about ten o'clock in clock terms, and I could feel its power and majesty even though I couldn't even see its outline in the night. Again, that alone would have made the experience worthwhile but as I sat there breathing softly and lowly a veritable parade of grazing and watering animals moved in and out of the light and shadow created by the Kilaguni's floodlights.

A few feet below me, several groups of animals came by feeding on the grasses beside the lodge. There were seven or eight waterbucks at one time and then part of a herd of water buffalo. It was thrilling. At one point I heard elephants trumpeting at the farthest waterhole. And all the while I continued to feel Kilimanjaro in the background, in the dark, unseen, but palpably there.

Finally, as it neared dawn, with the bright Milky Way fading into the first hints of day, I observed a group of three elephants interacting some forty or fifty yards away from me. It was incredible. Until the sun came up and they moved on, first for another drink of water and then into the plains beyond the lodge and out of sight, these elephants communicated with each other in a way I had not expected.

They made soft rumbling noises, short little sounds, talking to one another as it were, all the while touching each other from time to time with their long, flexible trunks. To me it seemed, for all the world, like three friends simply relaxing and visiting. Chatting casually while the world rested and the pressure of day-to-day survival was for the moment put on hold. An admixture of joy and melancholy coursed through me as these beasts finally took their leave with the coming of the day. I missed them immediately. I will never forget them and the way they spoke back and forth, the way they expressed obvious affection for each other. They were truly beautiful.

Finally, as the sun rose and Kilimanjaro came fully back into view and the Marrabou stork (whose awful visage seemed like that of something a thousand years old) floated awkwardly in to drink at the water holes, I rose, stretched, and went back into the room.

I didn't say anything about the experience to anyone. I slid back into bed and lay there silently recalling and absorbing my night on the balcony. I kept the memory to myself, hoarded it. It was mine and mine alone. No one needed to know about it until I was ready to share. Some things you like to keep to yourself, you know, at least for a while anyway. In this case, for a long while.

I Wish I Had Bought That Big Knife in Isiolo

WE LEFT NAIROBI about seven-thirty on a sunny Saturday morning. Our guide was a tour driver who called himself "Captain" Williams and he had christened his open-air flatbed truck the "Ark." Captain Williams's claim to fame, as we quickly learned, was that back in the sixties sometime he had been the guide for none other than Lucy Baines Johnson.

In my group, ferried along the pencil-thin roads of Kenya by the redoubtable Captain Williams, were two young British men, traveling separately, a couple from Australia, a mid-twenties American oil field worker from Saudi Arabia who was treating his younger brother to the trip of a lifetime, and a Canadian couple.

Although the day-long journey from Nairobi to Samburu was on roads best described as lane-and-a-half blacktop, the captain drove in a manner best described as erratic and frequently dangerous. At a reckless pace showing little concern for oncoming vehicles, the captain whipped his big truck around, in, and out of whatever traffic presented itself along the way to the Northern Territory where Jomo Kenyatta had been exiled for leading the Mau Mau uprisings of the 1950s.

Along the way we passed several coffee farms, a huge pineapple field, and many waving children. We traveled through rolling hills dotted with small banana plantations, stopped briefly at the colorful marketplace in Karatina, and eventually climbed out of the hills and onto a plateau. By midday, Mount Kenya loomed up to our right, and we stopped for lunch at a picnic and camping spot with a nice view of the impressive 17,000 feet high landmark.

After our meal, we went on to the equator where a handful of native craftsmen sold wooden animals and other touristy things out of a group of small kiosks at the side of the road. In mid-afternoon we stopped at the Marina Hotel and Bar in Nanyuku for some refreshing drinks and a brief rest before buying a couple of cases of Tusker Lager, a local beer, to take with us for drinking in camp.

Later in the day we reached Isiolo, gateway to the Samburu wild animal preserve and the Northern Territory, and we picked up a few items from a small supermarket near the center of town. Isiolo struck me as more of an Arab town than an African one and the numbers of Arab-looking people and the presence of many camels certainly added to that impression.

More than anything, though, I felt that Isiolo was a town without law. There was an odd atmosphere to the place, something hinting at an unspoken criminality and danger. I kept my thoughts to myself for fear of appearing too paranoid, but I was barely able to restrain myself from buying a large knife from a young street hawker as the truck pulled out of town for Samburu. It was a decision I would later regret, but I didn't know that quite yet.

Over bumpy, dusty dirt roads, then, we finally reached Samburu with enough light left to make a late, short game run before going on to our campsite. The overwhelming and immediate impression we got of the area was that of a land under stress from the drought that had plagued Kenya then for nearly seven years.

Far worse than what I had seen at Amboseli and Tsavo West in southeast Kenya the week before, the land of Samburu was dry, brown, and parched. The loose, cracked soil swept up and away by

swirling wind and dust devil. The animals reflected their harsh environment. They were gray and brown and jittery, their bodies emaciat-
ed, ribs sticking out flagrantly in overt testimony to the dire circumstances in which they labored simply to stay alive.

We arrived at our tented camp above a small stream around six
p.m. and settled in after our long day of traveling. Two Masai guards,
far afield there in the north, appeared in a jeep and helped the captain prepare supper. In the distance as we ate, to the northeast, there
were flashes of lightning that illuminated towering cumulus clouds.
It reminded me of our flight from London to Nairobi where, in the
restive early morning hours, I had seen a similar sight from the safety
of perhaps a hundred miles or more, a huge electrical storm lighting
up the clouds over North Africa.

As I sat there relaxing, I recalled some of the major events of my
first week in Kenya. In Nairobi, my first images were of streets filled
with masses of people walking, walking to work, walking hand in
hand, walking everywhere it seemed. And there had been many crip-
ples, their arms and legs twisted by diseases long conquered in the
so-called "first" world.

From Nairobi the group I was with that week had headed off in a
Volkswagen van for the Amboseli lodge and game preserve southeast
of Nairobi. At Amboseli we entered through the Mananga gate with
Mount Meru rising up out of the Tanzanian plains in the distance to
our right. When we reached the Amboseli Lodge, the clouds covering
nearby Mount Kilimanjaro lifted to reveal Kibo and Mawenzi peaks,
and on our first afternoon game drive we came across a herd of elephants that included close to fifty individuals.

After Amboseli came Tsavo West, where along the way we visited a Masai village whose men, to my delight and in a display
of Masai enthusiasm and aggressiveness, gathered around me and
thrust their spears in a semi-circle at my feet. I bought two of the
spears on the spot.

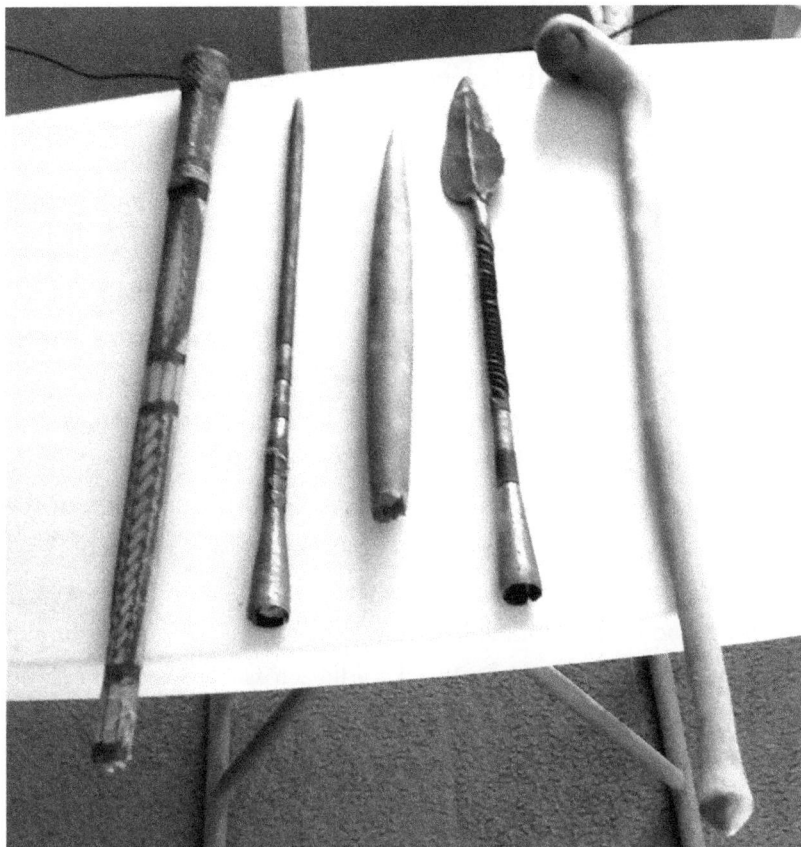

Left to right: knife from Isiolo, Kenya; Masai Spear, in 3 parts; Masai cowherd club, purchased in Kenya, 1984.
Photo by J. B. Hogan

After two pleasant days at Tsavo West, we returned to Nairobi where I rested up for the trip to Samburu in the barren north. The first night at the camp in Samburu turned out to be a memorable one. I had finally fallen asleep after the tiring travel day and felt like I had just closed my eyes when some noise in the camp woke me up.

One of the British guys was out in the middle of camp crying out that he had been robbed at spear point. In a moment the entire camp turned out and the captain came hustling up with the Masai guards.

The Aussie couple and the American oil field worker breathlessly told of being robbed, too. The Captain sent the Masai guards off in search of the thieves and insisted that the Aussie guy and the American go with him in the truck to report the incident to local authorities.

Taking the two men with him, the captain cranked up his truck and in what seemed like mere seconds the three of them roared out of camp. They traveled on a rutted road that led from the campsite through the brush and trees up a winding hill leading to a narrow strip of pavement that ran from the preserve back to Isiolo.

In a matter of only a few minutes, we had learned that we had been robbed, most likely by local tribesmen, and were now, those of us who remained in camp that is, completely alone. Without the captain there was no transportation nor was there any means of communication out in the middle of nowhere in the Samburu reserve.

We stood there stunned, listening to the grinding and belching of the big truck whose lights bounced wildly across the desert-like scrub beside the road. We watched the lights go straight out from the site, then slowly turn in a clockwise semi-circle until they made a sharp right that paralleled the encampment. In what seemed like less than a heartbeat, the truck had disappeared into the Kenyan night.

For several minutes after the guards and the men and the truck had vanished into the black night, the camp was silent, each of us remaining there allowing the sudden events to sink in. No one made even a gesture of venturing beyond the established area of the tents.

For me, those first few moments made me feel painfully alone, tiny in the vast African landscape, and completely vulnerable. I immediately started trying to organize the camp. First I tried to find anything that could be used as a weapon. The robbers might come back, I reasoned, and who knew where they had come from or gone to. What I found in the way of weaponry was a broken shovel handle and the short end of an old, rusted hoe. They seemed better than nothing.

We gathered up all the lamps we had in camp and then collected wood to build a large fire in an existing rock circle previously used for the same purpose. We broke out a box of "biscuits" and made a large pot of tea.

Over the next few dark hours, with no one able to get more than a quick cat nap for rest, we checked the camp perimeter every quarter of an hour or so. Despite our concern and frequent reconnoitering of camp, the slow moving time passed uneventfully, until around four in the morning.

The camp had fallen silent for some time, as most of us had drifted into a torpid state between sleep and waking. Suddenly, lights appeared in the brush beyond camp. We all leapt up.

"See those lights?" Someone asked. "Over there. See them?"

"I see them." I grabbed up the partial shovel and wielded it like a metal bat.

We formed into a loose circle at the head of camp, waiting for whomever was behind those lights. And the lights kept coming closer, jogging up and down like big, scary fireflies. We moved closer together. The lights kept coming. But then another light appeared. Farther out, to the right of camp, up on a distant rise.

"They're coming back." Someone else cried out. "Look. It's the truck. It's the captain."

"Yeah." I lowered the shovel. "Oh, yeah."

"It's the guards." Another person spoke, as the bobbing lights were revealed to be the lanterns carried by the long-missing Masai security team.

"They saw the captain's light. They were hiding out in the bush waiting for him to get back."

Captain Williams's return was a showy event, one met with considerable joy and relief. The Brit and the American were greeted as long lost prodigals and the three policemen they brought along with them as conquering heroes. Tea was reheated and biscuits offered and accepted by the returning men and their cadre of well-armed officers.

The Captain spoke briefly to the Masai guards and then they and the police made a brief search of the area, though it was still too dark for them to find any lost items or to stray more than a few yards away from the camp. Nonetheless, the presence of the police and the safe return of our two men was enough to calm the group, and we retired to our tents to get a little rest before the morning's first game drive, which the captain insisted we do regardless of what had happened.

Before the morning drive could get underway, however, around seven-thirty, a squad of Kenyan soldiers rumbled up to camp in a dusty Land Rover. They were carrying .303 British Enfield rifles and immediately set about investigating the robbery with detached efficiency. Somewhere down by the small creek that ran below camp, the soldiers found some pieces of clothing and the Aussie girl's glasses, fortunately unbroken, by a clump of bushes beyond the creek.

After completing their work, the soldiers explained to us that the thieves were from a local tribe known for preying upon vulnerable tourists. The soldiers informed us that the camp had been robbed several times in succession over the past few months.

The difference in this case was the beer. The tribesmen had discovered our stash where we left it cooling down by the small creek and they drank all of it. The result was they were emboldened to make a direct robbery rather than the raid that usually took place while unsuspecting tourists like us were out on a game drive.

"Yes, well," the captain responded to our somewhat heated questioning, "they usually cut holes in the back of the tents and take what they want that way. I fear this time they became overly brave by drinking the beer you left outside camp. Come along now, it's time for the morning drive."

Shaking our heads, we followed the captain to his truck. The Masai guards waved to us as we climbed on board the big flatbed for another spectacular game drive in Kenya's far north country. In minutes the robbery was forgotten as the group, our spirits buoyed by the sight of so many exotic animals thin though they may have been from the drought, allowed itself to be won over by the abundance of life that still remained in Samburu.

Mid-morning, after the game drive, we packed up our belongings, those who still had them that was, and piled back into the captain's big truck for the trip down to Lake Nakuru, our next stop. On the way out, we again passed through Isiolo and this time when the boys hawked their long knives, I immediately snatched one up.

For the remainder of the tour the knife was never far from my side, including the three days and nights we spent camped beside a small stream in the vast grasslands of the Masai Mara. In fact, I held onto that knife all the way back to the states, packing it carefully inside my checked baggage. Today, decades later, the knife is rusted and dull but I still have it. I'm not planning to get rid of it any time soon, either. No, sir, that knife is going nowhere, it stays with me forever.

Some of Us in Tucson Didn't Like the War in Central America

FOR MUCH OF the 1980s while the United States waged a surrogate war via the Contras (or counter revolutionaries) against the leftist Sandinista government of Nicaragua some of us didn't agree with this approach and openly protested against it. My friend Tom and I joined a group called the Tucson Committee for Human Rights in Latin America (TCHRLA—pronounced Chur-la for short).

We would meet from time to time to discuss ways to protest the war and how we could support the people of Nicaragua. We noticed in the group that there were several types of progressives (some people might substitute the word radical here). There were old school peace and love hippies—they ran around with colorful banners and such and seemed disconnected from the political side of the situation. We, as in my buddy and I, didn't take them seriously.

There were ardent, and also old school, Marxist-Leninists as well who tended to be super political and usually lacked much of a sense of humor, of which Tom and I probably had too much. Some of these folks were members of the Communist Party but because the CP was outlawed in the state of Arizona, they called their organization People Before Profits. We had religious people in the group, too, many of them sincerely opposed to war instead of its less violent alternative, diplomacy.

One member of our group, who edited our little newsletter, would later become a well-known writer and that was Barbara King-solver. I don't know if she has ever mentioned it in her work or not but she was part of the group back in those days. Her novel Animal Dreams has some characters based on a couple of the people who were in or connected to TCHRLA.

So, we used to have large (and small) protests around Tucson. Marching up Speedway Boulevard, gathering in parks afterward for fellowship, food, and—if we could get past the M-L guardians—fun. One thing that tickled me was that one guy in the group liked to call me, humorously, Comandante Jerry. This always amused me greatly and I always thought it was funny even if tinged with more than a tad of sarcasm.

I was a part of TCHRLA, even if peripherally, and I wrote an article or two for their newsletter, but as the decade of the eighties wound down I drifted and then moved away from group involvement—consciously reducing my involvement in protest politics. But not before taking some memorable trips to Central America and Mexico.

Whoa, Oh, Sandinista

N OT QUITE A year after my African adventure, in the spring of 1985, I made my first trip to Central America. I went to study Spanish and to see the Sandinista revolution up close and personal.

I had recently gotten back from an IBM work trip to Boeblingen Lab in Germany (near Stuttgart) and was anxious to do something that was personally and politically satisfying to me. As described earlier, I had been a peripheral figure in the Tucson progressive movement scene and wanted to crown my numerous stateside meetings, rallies, and demonstrations with a visit to the real thing—Sandinista Nicaragua. I wanted to see for myself what such a world would be like.

After taking an absolutely maxed out milk run flight from Tucson to Mexico City (four intermediate stops along the way) on Aero-Mexico, I flew Taca (the El Salvadoran airline) first to the heavily-armed and -guarded San Salvador airport and then on to Managua. In Managua's Augusto Sandino Airport a picture of Sandino himself complete with Tom Mix cowboy hat greeted me. Shortly after my arrival, Barbara, a representative of the language school I was going to attend, and Lillian, a young woman from Tucson and dedicated progressive, did the same.

After getting me through the maze of airport customs, my hosts took me and several other new arrivals on a school bus to Barrio Maximo Jerez and got us settled in with the families we would be staying with while in Managua. My family, Esperanza and Julio, lived in a smallish sort of ramshackle house with mostly dirt floors and the most rudimentary bathroom and cooking facilities I'd seen since I was kid out in the country in the Arkansas Ozarks.

I had a small, narrow room off to the right side of the front door with two cots in it. I took the cot on the left and for my entire three-week stay in Managua I had the room to myself, a definite bonus. There was no hot water in the tiny bathroom located near the head of my cot and occasionally huge water bugs would hop around in there like some kind of weird giant grasshoppers or something. I wasn't too keen on the water bugs.

After a couple of days of orientation, lots of political meetings and explanations of Sandinista positions on various topics, I started school at the Casa Nicaraguense de Español (CNE). The school was in a one-story house in a tree-filled neighborhood not terribly far from downtown Managua. You could walk downtown without that much exertion.

Overall, CNE was a good experience. I made many new friends there and it was my home base over the next weeks. It is difficult to summarize the trip because so many events, people, and situations stand out. Still, these are some of the main experiences I took away from that first visit.

Week one. Managua was the poorest larger city I had ever been in. Somoza, Jr. had emptied the state treasury when he fled the country and that left the new government with not much more than ideals to finish off the political side of their revolution. I mentioned that my family had dirt floors, no hot water, and fairly unsanitary living conditions. On the streets I saw buses so overcrowded the tires were almost flat. I saw many horse-drawn carts, some even with wooden wheels, and consumer goods were practically non-existent.

Local campesino band, El Coral, Nicaragua, Spring 1985.
J. B. Hogan Collection

Although it was a trivial matter, beer, for example, was not easy to
come by and you had to drink it at a bar (the one we frequented was
El Radial) unless you brought a container of your own for carry-outs.
Sodas were sold in plastic bags with a straw stuck into them, bottles
being at an absolute premium. The official unit of currency, the Cor-
doba, was kept artificially over-valued against the dollar (28 to 1) and
what you could buy was unnecessarily expensive.

There were two major *mercados* (markets) in town, the govern-
ment-approved Roberto Huembes and the unapproved black market
Oriental. At the Oriental, it was rumored, you could get as many as
500 cordobas for the dollar. There were several supermarkets in town
but they literally had nothing in them. I mean nothing.

On my first Saturday, I went with a school outing to a country
village called El Coral at the edge of the war zone. There was some
Contra activity in the area and once we got well out in the country
we picked up a Sandinista soldier, with AK-47 in hand, as our guard.

If it hadn't been for the onset of Somoza's Revenge, I would have enjoyed myself at El Coral. There was a *campesino* band, food and drink, a political rally and a rodeo. There were only outhouses there in the country and you had to battle past various farm animals, including some large and aggressive pigs, to make it to the bathroom. Overall, it was an entertaining day.

Sunday, my new friend Jeff and I took a bus from Roberto Huembes market over to the town of Grenada where we walked down to Puerto Asese at the shore of Lake Nicaragua. We drank beer at an outdoor bar, relaxed, and listened to the complaints of a drunken Miskito Indian kid who had been drafted into the Army even though he was totally anti-Sandinista.

Week two. The Revenge eased up a little and we continued learning about the country's history and culture, the recent revolution, and what the political scene consisted of at the moment. We remained regulars at El Radial, beer is always especially tasty on these long trips, and on Friday we took off on another school trip.

This time we drove over toward the east coast to the city of León, passing recently picked cotton fields and a gigantic, smoking volcano along the way. In town, we were led by a Sandinista guide and watched Good Friday processions through the streets and up to a small field where the passion of Calvary was replayed (with considerable intensity, I might add).

Later we drove on to the beach at Poneloya where we drank some cool beer. I body surfed there but several of us felt guilty about having fun at the beach while young Nicaraguan soldiers were fighting and dying in the different war zones around the country. We arrived back in Managua as a huge, full moon was rising, the image stuck in my mind and became the first lines of a poem that I would later write about this and my second trip to the country.

Saturday we went to the beach at Pochomil where we (my new buds Chris and Andres, nee Andrew) drank more beer, felt less guilty about the war and relaxed. On Sunday I rested my Revenge at home with my family and read (upon the recommendation of my new friend Carol) *Dance the Eagle to Sleep,* a fine 60s novel by the fine novelist Marge Piercy.

Week three. I discovered that AeroMexico had canceled my entire return flight because they had unilaterally decided I failed to make the trip down in the first place, huh? Most of this week was spent trying to get my flights out of country arranged. On Friday, I got lucky and ran into my friend Lillian near the Hotel Intercontinental and was able to say goodbye to her.

On Saturday I flew Aeronica (known locally as Aeronunca, a local joke, translating to "Never Flies") to Mexico City and after a brief ordeal caught a Mexicana flight to Los Angeles. Within an hour of my re-arrival in the States, I was suffering major culture shock by having an expensive veggie burger at Larry Parker's, a trendy restaurant in Beverly Hills. The intellectual and emotional wrenching of being in poor Nicaragua in the morning and in Beverly Hills the same evening was almost more than I was ready for.

The next morning, I flew out of the Burbank Airport to Phoenix and then on down to Tucson. I caught a ride from the Tucson Airport and my first trip to Central America was officially over.

July 19, 1985
Nicaragua Party

A COUPLE OF months after my return from Nicaragua, on July 19, 1985, several local progressive groups in Tucson put together a fund-raising party at the Splinter Brothers and Sisters Warehouse night club. The aim was to celebrate July 19, 1979, the date of the Sandinista victory, by raising money to send down to the poor, cash-strapped Central American country.

My friend Tom was in charge of getting the club where we held the dance, the drinks, alcoholic and otherwise, and five or six Tucson bands, who played—to their credit—for free. The evening was a smashing success. We made a bundle of money for the cause (I can't remember exactly anymore but it was up around one thousand dollars) and had a serious party, as well.

Anyone and everyone in town who had any political awareness of any kind was there that night. The atmosphere was loose and open, people were happy, people were a little tipsy, the bands rocked on, and people were dancing all over the place. It kind of had the joyousness of old 60s-type get togethers. Though busy some of the night working as a volunteer, I had a fun time. I was only three months back from the trip to Central America and so the feelings and meaning of the evening ran deeply within me. But it was also true that I got drunker than a skunk. I was having a blast.

There were lots of good-looking women there, naturally, and I danced with several of them. In the course of the evening, as I got more and more inebriated I lost most of my inhibitions and was flinging myself around the sawdust floor in front of the bands with wild abandon. I was about to turn forty, but I felt like a kid. I was, for that night, happy and unrestrained.

When the evening finally wound down and I was ready to go home, Barbara Kingsolver and Joe, her husband then, were concerned about my drunken state.

"Are you sure you're okay to drive?" They pleaded with me not to take off in my old rundown Toyota Corolla.

"I'm okay." I waved them off. Of course, I absolutely was not all right, and I'm lucky I didn't get pulled over because I would have been DUI without doubt.

"You're sure, now?"

"Oh, yeah, I'm okay. I can drive fine."

"You know we could take you home and you can come get your car in the morning."

"Naw, I'll be all right. No problem."

"Please be careful, then."

"I'll be careful."

I drove off then and made it home fine. No DUI. No accidents. No problems. I was plain lucky.

We had another party the next year on July 19, 1986, but it didn't match up to this one. All the same elements were in place but repeating anything, even or perhaps especially a party or celebration, is virtually impossible to do. I would find the same thing out a few years later in Mexico when I tried to relive my first big trip down there. You can't catch lightning in a bottle twice no matter who you are. At least I can't, anyway.

The Israeli Girl I Thought
Was a Spanish Actress
(She Thought I Was CIA)

IN THE FALL of 1987 I made a second trip to Nicaragua. This time I was part of an international group sent to provide technical support at different agencies and the like around Managua and out in the country. I worked for *Barricada Internacional,* the English-language world-distributed version of the Sandinista newspaper.

I was supposed to help the newspaper convert from old typesetting equipment to personal computers but due to limited resources and my limited knowledge of PCs in those days, I ended up only doing some typesetting and a bit of minor translating. What I mostly did was work on my own fiction writing.

I hadn't been back in Managua long on this trip when I came down with a strong flu. I mean I was flat on my back, fever, headache, all the good stuff. I remember lying there in my little cot, feeling the wonderfully warm and refreshing tropical air wafting over my overheated body. I could hear the big parrots outside the room chattering away and I could hear the other members of the Tecnica group coming and going. Occasionally someone would come by to check on me but they mostly, and properly, left me alone.

One afternoon as I lay there in my little pool of fever sweat seeing the world through a reddish flu haze, I heard some kind of commotion outside. I turned on my left side to try and look out one of the windows in my room to see what was up. I couldn't see very well but I managed to catch a glimpse of a young woman outside and that was enough. She was absolutely beautiful. So much so in fact, that in my feverish state I managed to concoct the idea that she must be a Spanish actress in some troupe stopping at our little way station for *internacionalistas.*

A day or so later, as I sat in a chair outside my room recuperating and reading *Gorky Park* by Martin Cruz Smith, this extraordinary vision appeared again. At least I knew she was real this time and not a figment of my burning imagination. Remarkably, she was even prettier than my previous glimpse had led me to believe and she was friendly. A couple of days later, at the bar El Chaguite, a local hang-out for international workers, I asked her name. It was a Jewish name and in my fervent, post-fever, best Marxist-Leninist idiocy, I asked, "Is that an Israeli name?"

An Israeli name? What kind of question was that? From what hidden depths of completely un-mined anti-Semitism did I dredge that sucker up from. Anti-Israeli government or Anti-militant Zionism is one thing, but jeez, what a dodo head.

Naturally this beautiful young woman bristled a bit at such a stupidly phrased question and I knew I'd blown it. Blown it big time. The next day we had a political argument and she all but accused me of being CIA. CIA? The worst possible thing you could be associated with down there. Naturally, after that we had nothing to say to one another. I had seen, met, become friendly with, super-annoyed, and completely alienated one of the best looking women I'd ever met all in the course of two short days. I suppose I've been stupider, but I sure don't remember when.

Other than that little episode, however, my second three-week visit went well. I made several new friends, got a lot of writing done, went on some weekend trips, including one to Matagalpa where we visited the grave of Ben Linder, an American killed by the Contras the year before, I believe it was. I generally learned more about the country, the difficulties and compromises required to keep a revolution going when the most powerful country in the world is trying to disrupt it. Does the word Cuba ring a bell here with anyone?

La Mordida at the Mexico City Airport

WHEN I RETURNED from Managua, I flew to Mexico City with a young woman named Becky from the Tecnica group. We decided to leave our few belongings in storage at the Mexico City airport. But when we went to pick them up a few days later before catching our return flights to the states I encountered what is known in Mexico as la mordida for the first time up close and personal.

La mordida is "the bite." It is how the Mexican economic system, a gigantic pyramid scheme, works. For example, the street corner cop hits you up for some imagined or real minor traffic violation, you give him x number of pesos. He then gives some portion of those x pesos to his immediate superior (who gathers them from all of his inferiors) and the bite continues on up the scale to the top of the government where the president sits in totally corrupt glory.

Some of the presidents, including Miguel de la Madrid and Carlos Salinas de Gortari for example, worked this system to such success that the former moved to France (at least for a while if not permanently) and the latter was forced to live several years in the United States for fear of extradition back to Mexico and certain prosecution.

Anyway, on the more local, personal level, *la mordida* is the bribe system used by authorities to enrich their own lives and that of their

bosses. Later, I would see la mordida in action on the highway between Mexico City and Cuernavaca. A Mexican highway patrol unit
was stopping all vehicles and demanding small amounts of pesos
from the drivers. But in 1987 I had only heard of it, not experienced
it yet. Until the Mexico City airport incident that is.

What happened was that when my friend and I went to get our
belongings, the two guards put the squeeze on us. I didn't get it at first,
my Spanish never being all that great, but it slowly began to sink in.

"Nuestras maletas estan alla." I was trying, in my poor Spanish,
to tell the guards that our bags had been stored back in the adjacent
locker area.

They said something I didn't understand but it was clear there was
no rush to find our bags. I tried again. Again I didn't understand them.

"What's wrong?" my friend asked, her Spanish being weaker
than mine.

"I'm not sure. They don't seem to want to get our bags."

"We've got to get them."

I nodded and tried again.

Finally, after a few attempts, I began to understand at least the
gist of what the guards were saying. They were telling me it cost some
number of pesos to retrieve our bags from the lockers. They were
smiling and laughing a little, as if the three of us understood some
kind of joke. To this day, I do not know how I finally caught on, but
I did. I understood that they were looking for a little money to get
our things. Nothing big. Something like a tip.

"Oh." I pulled a few thousand pesos out of my pocket (the exchange rate then was about 2270 pesos to the dollar) and handed it
to the guards. *"Un regalito para café."* I tried to deflect the idea that I
was bribing them. "A little gift for coffee."

The guards nodded and smiled and almost immediately went
back and got our bags. We parted on good terms and Becky and I
hustled to catch our flights.

"That was it." I commented as we walked through the airport. *"La mordida.* The bite."

"I am so glad you understood." She made me feel all streetwise and experienced. "I would've never known what they wanted, what the problem was."

"I don't know how I did, either." I admitted. "But it worked. We're outta there."

"Thanks a lot." She smiled at me. "You saved us."

"You're welcome." I beamed. "Glad it worked out."

I saw her to her plane and as is so common in these travel situations, I never heard from or saw her again. It was only a little moment in time, one between two people traveling in the same part of the world far away from their own homes and culture. In my own experience, it was the kind of little moment that seemed to happen in every longer trip, the kind that makes that trip memorable, even fun to remember, and totally worth having done.

Quitting IBM—
Can You Do That?

FTER MY SECOND trip to Nicaragua, I was determined to save some money, quit IBM, and go to Mexico. Mexico, which was vastly richer than poor little Nicaragua, seemed like it would be a place where I could get away from things for a while. This might seem like an odd statement, but after seeing the poverty of Nicaragua, Mexico seemed like a true paradise to me.

I worried my last few months at IBM that they were going to promote me and so make me feel committed to them and stay longer. Luckily, that didn't happen and in February of 1988 I quit IBM in order to head south of the border.

The funniest part of my leaving IBM was the meeting called by my manager to announce to the other employees that I was quitting to pursue a different life, at least for the time being. The manager, a decent guy, had tried hard to get me to take a leave of absence, not quit, but I insisted on resigning. I had to make a clean break (this insistence of mine would later cost me about $100,000 in a buy out that occurred sometime in the summer of 1988, but that's a whole other story).

At the announcement meeting, our manager generously went through some of the things I had done for the department and so on and then finally came to the point of the gathering.

J. B. Hogan at work, Tucson, AZ, 1987.
J. B. Hogan Collection

"Jerry has decided to quit IBM." He informed my mostly surprised co-workers. "He'll be pursuing other interests outside the company. We wish him the best in his future endeavors and thank him for his work here."

There was a kind of general buzzing around the room and a couple of guffaws from my closest friends and then one of the guys, a graphic artist with a darned good sense of humor, leaned over toward me and said in a voice loud enough for all to hear.

"Can you do that? Can you quit IBM?"

The room broke up laughing, especially me. It was the perfect note to sound at the time and it comically reflected the attitudes of IBMers in those days. This was still the era of Big Blue Momma, when the company tried to make it seem like they were the workers' protection from cradle to grave. Some of us never bought into that philosophy, but many of the IBMers, especially old- and long-timers did and had for years. Not being one of those folks, however, I did quit and in what seemed like an extraordinarily short period of time found myself south of the border, deep in the heart of Old Mexico itself.

What the Heck
Did I Just Do?

FROM THE OUTDOOR patio café inside the Papagayo Hotel compound two blocks south of the main bus station in Cuernavaca the large multicolored neon sign parrot that was the hotel's symbol hovered over the driveway of the midscale establishment in the heart of the city of Eternal Spring. I was having a Corona beer and trying to figure out what exactly it was that I had done. What was I doing sitting here at the Papagayo, casually sipping a brew when I had quit a perfectly good, well-paying permanent job back in Tucson?

I had known I was going to quit my job since my second trip to Central America in the fall of 1987. Having seen Mexico City a second time, the first had been my initial trip back in the spring of 1985, I had determined, after seeing the poverty of Nicaragua, that Mexico was a hugely richer country and a much better place to escape from the United States for a while. Still, knowing all this, I had a moment there at the Papagayo, a moment when I had to ask myself a simple question, what in the world had I done?

The next morning, as I adjusted to the thicker humidity, the thinner air, and the steamier heat of Cuernavaca, I caught a cab up to the language school that would be the base of my operations for the next six weeks.

Centro Bilingue Language School, Cuernavaca, Morelos, Mexico, Spring 1988.
J. B. Hogan Collection

The school, Centro Bilingüe, did not disappoint. The grounds of the school were green and lush with many unfamiliar but beautiful flowers of red and yellow and many shades in between. The school was laid out in a kind of extended L-shape with a brown stucco classroom building on your immediate left as you entered the grounds. Down a set of wide steps inside and to your left was a small vending area serving soft drinks and snacks.

A little farther up to the right was a two-story classroom and straight in was the administration building. Making a left by the admin building you climbed steps up to several more classroom buildings, the on-site doctor's office (the old, probably no longer licensed doctor dispensed considerable advice on avoiding Montezuma's revenge, the tourist's main enemy).

Behind everything, *al fondo* (out back in Spanish), was the *alber-*

ca, the swimming pool. All in all, with its clean, colorful buildings, efficient staff, and incredibly beautiful grounds, Centro Bilingüe was a fine place to study and learn Spanish.

If Mexico Sucks So Bad, Then Why Are We All Down Here?

G IVEN THE CURRENT climate in Mexico, what with all the drug crime, killings, kidnappings, and such, it might seem stupid to talk about what a great place it is and maybe that's true. But in the late 80s and early 90s things weren't as bad as they have been these last few years. In some places maybe, but not all over.

Of course, there has always been an attitude in the U.S. about how crappy it is below the border. You know, backward, poor, dirty, blah, blah, blah. Well, corrupt government and this exploding drug war aside, Mexico was and is a beautiful, resource-rich nation. It has an extraordinary, if tumultuous, history and is filled with interesting people to meet and amazing places to see.

Shortly after I began to study Spanish, and Mexican history and culture at the Centro Bilingüe language school, I began to make friends. Most of the school's students were college kids from the U.S. but there were older students, too, and most of my new friends came from this group.

Among them was Jim, a smooth, well-dressed reporter for the *Los Angeles Times*; Katrina, a mid-thirties blonde who worked for the Bank of America in San Francisco; Lucy, a dark-haired nurse from somewhere also in California; and Celia, a newly-graduated doctor

Bar Universal, Cuernavaca, Morelos, Mexico, Spring 1988.
Internet Image

from UCLA who would become my closest friend. In addition to this group, we had our friends from across the pond as well, new acquaintances Tomas and Kris, from Norway and Germany, respectively, as well as a number of others who floated in and out on the winds of chance and opportunity.

After classes, we often congregated at an open-air bar and restaurant across from Cuernavaca's jardín, or central plaza, called the Bar Universal, sipping on sodas or beers and chatting about our lives. Most everyone in the group seemed to be getting over a recent relationship. That sort of thing seemed to be common in Mexico and nearly everyone at the table admitted to such as well.

In the course of our discussion someone had been griping about Mexico, maybe they had run up against its maddening bureaucracy or something like that, and several others joined in to voice complaints against our host nation. Most of these complaints had at least a bit of truth to them, but I remember it struck me as a little hypocritical that most of us, close to one hundred percent, were down there for the same reason, getting over the end of a love affair that had gone bad. Mexico had been the choice of country in which to do the forgetting and recovering and yet there we were griping our little heads off about it.

"You know, guys," I finally said at one point, "if Mexico sucks so bad, then why are we all down here? Anybody got an idea on that?"

There was a long pause in the conversation. We all looked at each other. I imagine they were doing the same thing I was. Thinking of this beautiful country, especially so down there in Cuernavaca, with its lush foliage, its air of hope and mystery, nearly palpable as dusk spread over us there at the café, and its exciting aura of future, happier potentiality. The pause continued for another moment or two as we reflected on our new circumstances and the choices that had brought us here.

Finally, someone broke the spell, spoke again. But we spoke more softly now and about other things. There were no more complaints about Mexico, no more gripes. We sat there and sipped on our drinks, feeling safe among new friends, happy in our new surroundings, hopeful about our individual futures, the beginning of which was now, here, in Old Mexico.

I've Never Been There and I'll Never Go Again

ONE OF THE reasons I chose to go to Mexico after I quit my job in Tucson, among many others, was that I wanted to see the ruins at Teotihuacan. I had been fascinated by Teotihuacan ever since I had seen it for the first time on some travelogue-like show probably on PBS back in the states.

I had been at Centro Bilingüe only a couple of weeks when one of the weekend school excursions was to the ruins outside Mexico City. I was probably the first person who signed up for the jaunt to Teotihuacan, and I was excited the entire trip from Cuernavaca to Mexico City and then on out into the desert valley where the mighty pyramids of the Sun and Moon stood in awesome splendor above the arid Mexican land.

On the way to the pyramids, even as we could see them in the distance, I got off one of my few jokes in Spanish. I had to ask our tour guide for help with the translation but in effect it went like this.

I was pretending that going to the ruins would be no big thing, so I asked the guide how to say something along the lines of, well, we can see the pyramids up ahead there, so there's no reason to go on any farther. Let's head back to school. The guide thought that was a funny concept, so he taught me a phrase in Spanish to cover such an absurdity.

"*Nunca he ido,*" our guide told me the expression was, "*y nunca volveré a ir!*"

When the driver started laughing, I figured we had hit on a fun wise guy expression.

"I've never been there," the phrase translates to, "and I'll never go again."

Perfect. I practiced it a couple of times and then laid it on my fellow touring students from Centro Bilingüe. It was a big hit, getting the amount of laughs I'd hoped for. I slapped open hands with the tour guide and settled back happily for the short remainder of our ride to the pyramids. It was my first big joke in Spanish.

All kidding aside, however, Teotihuacan did not disappoint. Except for maybe all the vendors who chased you around among the restored and semi-restored buildings of the ancient, millennia-plus long dead former inhabitants of this impressive locale, hawking their cheap wares as if they were original pieces of Meso-American art. That little annoyance aside, Teo was great.

We crossed the wide Avenue of the Dead beyond the entrance to the archaeological zone and walked through the Ciudadela area, a series of facing, short flat-topped pyramids, on our way to the "new" Pyramid within an older Pyramid of Quetzalcoatl, chief god of the Teos.

Weaving our way back between the vendors to the Avenue of the Dead, we slowly traversed that long, dusty road running the entire length of the site which went past the Pyramid of the Sun and on to the Pyramid of the Moon at the far end of the wide path.

Jim, my reporter friend, and I decided to climb the Pyramid of the Sun, a somewhat daunting physical task. It is a tall pyramid with narrow steps leading to the summit. The view from the top is magnificent, of course, as you get a three-hundred and sixty-degree view of the area, including seeing the Pyramid of the Moon off to your right when you get to the top of the Pyramid of the Sun and face the stairs you just climbed up.

Climbing down the Pyramid of the Sun, now that's another thing altogether. The bottom looks so far away, so far below you. And the steps, oh boy, they look so narrow going down that it looks like if you slipped on one step you would fall all the way, step by step, hundreds of feet to the ground below. Going carefully, of course, you make it back down to the Avenue of the Dead just fine. A deep breath and you're off to the Pyramid of the Moon.

My friends and I didn't climb very far up the Pyramid of the Moon after that, even though it is much lower than the Pyramid of the Sun. We settled for a feel of how difficult it would be, the steps are much taller and wider than at the Pyramid of the Sun, and we soon came down to finish visiting the last few smaller ruins in the area.

We hit the trinket shops on the way out and rejoined our tour group at the bus. There is a *pulquería* on the grounds at Teotihuacan and I tried to get my pals to go there but they chose not to and so I missed that opportunity to sample the first step in the process of making tequila.

Teotihuacan is not, of course, the only set of ruins in Mexico and to some people it is secondary not only to Palenque but to Chichen Itza and even Tuluum. For my money, it's main rivals were Xochi-calco, out in the middle of the desert-like terrain to the southwest of Cuernavaca, and Monte Alban, the ruin in the mountains above Oaxaca in the southeast part of lower central Mexico. Travelers in the region often insist that the best ruins anywhere are at Tikal down in Guatemala. I never made it there but the pictures I've seen of Tikal make this claim seem solid. It looks fantastic.

A few weeks after my first trip to Teo, I replayed the visit and acted as tour guide for my doctor friend Celia. We had a terrific day there and she was so inspired by the sights that she wrote a poem. Her poem, in turn, triggered a poem of my own, which I wrote some weeks later when I was in the Yucatan waiting for her to return to Mexico after she had briefly gone back to California.

Before all that took place, however, there was still plenty of living to do in Cuernavaca, the living enhanced by the coterie of new friends I continued to make at Centro Bilingüe, including my German buddy Kris, more about whom follows.

Never Teach Your German Buddy American Slang

ONE OF THE best things about going to the language school in Cuernavaca was making new friends. Quite a few of those friends were from Europe and one of them, Kris, a German journalist who later would be a successful television personality in his home country, became a real buddy.

We hit the bars in Cuernavaca together, hammering down the huge *Tongoleles* (large mugs of beer) at the Bar Universal next to the *jardín*, and several other local watering holes. Invariably we would attend classes the next day feeling quite *"crudo"* (hungover) and our teachers teased us about our nightly excursions.

Kris had spent some time in Florida in years past and knew English quite well but he was absolutely voracious in his quest to learn our slang terms, as all motivated students of another language should be. He was always grilling me about such terms and one day I taught him a word that, to us southerners at least, is a funny one. The word is poontang. You can look it up if you don't know what it refers to.

He was so happy to learn this, at least to him, obscure Americanism that he soon took to using it all the time, sometimes almost like it was a term of greeting. He used it correctly and he used it incorrectly, but he used it a lot. He even got to calling me this word, which I had to try and explain to him made no sense whatsoever.

It's hard sometimes for enthusiastic foreigners to understand the subtleties of such fine colloquialisms. Lord only knows if he took the term back to Germany and who knows what his German friends would have thought of such an American slang term if he did. But the episode has always made me laugh when I think about it and I was pleased years later to learn of my friend's successful life in his native land.

After we parted ways in Cuernavaca, I never heard anything about him until I "Googled" his name not long ago and found out about his TV career. We exchanged a few friendly e-mails and I reminded him of the partying days in Cuernavaca and the slang word he learned back then. We both got a laugh out of that, even after all this time.

The Beach, The Doors, and Two Topless Girls

IN THE SPRING of 1988, after six weeks of studying Spanish in Cuernavaca, a large group of us, including most of my new-found friends, finished our courses and were ready to head back to the states or onto other travel adventures. Celia, for example, had to finish up some testing or do something related to landing her first internship as a doctor back in California. Lucy was going to Cuba as part of a medical tour. Kris was heading back home to Germany and everyone else I knew was off to wherever their lives would lead them. For me that next step would be a trip out to the Yucatan, where I would meet Lucy upon her return from Cuba and wait for Celia's return from the states.

I flew Mexicana out to Merida, the beautiful capital city of Yucatan state. Merida has two memorable features. One is a beautiful *jardín* or plaza (also called a *zocalo*) filled with meticulously trimmed trees and surrounded by open-air cafés on the north side of the park and by businesses and government buildings on the remaining sides.

The second striking thing about the city is that the streets are numbered, not named. That's right, Merida uses mostly numbers for its streets. One of my favorite things was near the *jardín* you could stand at the corner of 61st and 61st or something close to that.

Maybe it was the corner of 61st and 62nd. Still, rather amusing, at least to me.

Lucy came back to Mexico a day or so after I got to Merida and I took a taxi out to the airport to meet her. Back in town we settled into our separate rooms in the cheap-o Hotel San Jose. She had picked up a bad cough while in Cuba so we tracked down a *farmacia* to get her some cold medicine and then we waited for a friend of hers, also a nurse, to arrive from San Francisco.

When we were all together, we hopped a bus from Merida, passing through Valladolid and by Chichen Itza, to Cancun. In Cancun, the three of us shared a room, three beds, and checked out the famous resort town.

We took a bus out to the touristy *Zona Hotelera* (Hotel Zone) to see where the fancy people stayed, then went back to Ciudad Cancun, more our speed, and ate at a local, authentic Mexican restaurant. The next morning we shared a cab with an American man down to the coast at Playa del Carmen, where another friend of my friends joined us from the states. The three women shared a larger cabana type cabin near the beach and I took up residence a block or so inland in one of some little *bandas* called *La Rana Cansada* or something like that, which as I recall, translated to The Tired or Lazy Frog.

This is how my days at Playa del Carmen went. Day one, things were going great. The three women and I played on the beach and drank beer at a restaurant/bar near the water. I was having so much fun that I didn't realize I was getting badly sunburned. One reason I didn't notice what I was doing was because that area of Playa del Carmen was a topless beach. Mostly American women cavorting about in the shallow water in such a manner caused my brain to cease functioning properly.

To finish me completely off, at one point early in the afternoon I went up to my *banda* briefly to retrieve something, maybe sunglasses, and when I returned to the beach towel upon which my three women friends sat, two of them had decided to go topless as well. Worst of all, my personal friend, Lucy, had now divested herself of her top. Uh-oh. What to do?

How can a guy like myself, who enjoys women so much, carry on a conversation with them when their breasts are looking me right in the face—or should I say, I'm looking straight at them? It wasn't easy, let me tell you. I did a lot of looking up at the palm trees, over at the restaurant, up at the sky. I stared out at the wide expanse of the ocean as if looking for and perhaps even expecting to see Cortes and his band of crazed *conquistadores* arrive at any moment. Luckily, the women shortly put their tops back on and the return of blood to my brain allowed me to more cogently react to my environment.

Unfortunately, this new cogency allowed me to realize that I had earlier sunburned myself quite badly while splashing around near the water's edge and my legs in particular were becoming bright red. By evening I was down and out. I was a lobster. I was burnt to a crisp and sick to go along with it.

The next two days were a feverish blur, with my friends occasionally checking in on me. Thankfully, the women mostly left me alone, going ahead on visits down to the ruins at Tuluum and such, while I lay in my *banda* feeling miserable.

One of the main things I remember from my two days and nights of sunburned hell is lying there in my *banda* late one evening, listening to the sounds of the little beach resort (it was little then, not so much anymore I understand). From somewhere not too distant I could hear the Doors playing on someone's radio or record player and I recall how that music and the undeveloped nature (at that time) of Playa, with kids sleeping in hammocks tied between palm trees, combined to create this feeling of being out of time, or more aptly, in another time.

The 1960s to be exact. I had not felt those sensations in years and as I heard Jim Morrison singing, I recalled what I now considered to be the good old days, when I was young and free and optimistic. For that night, I felt the past again come alive and it was a pleasant feeling, tinged with a fair-sized amount of melancholy, to remember the days that used to be.

Finally, after a couple of lousy days sweating in my crappy little banda, I was well enough to carefully don my blue jeans, which rubbed painfully against my super tender skin with each cautious step and go back to Merida. My three women friends followed in a later bus and we rendezvoused once again, this time at a veggie restaurant near the *jardín* in Merida.

The following day I helped Lucy and the other nurse get to the airport for their flights out of town. The third woman had immediately left for somewhere else almost as soon as we got back to Merida. When all of my friends were safely away, I spent another painful day or two in town.

Finally, I boarded a Mexicana flight and made the return trip to Mexico City. My legs still hurt a lot, and I was now getting the full-blown flu, but I reasoned that I would soon be in a comfortable room in the Monte Carlo and that Celia would be back down to take care of me.

With much more of a whimper than any sort of a bang, my big trip to the Yucatan, where I had been given a body whupping by the sun, was over. It was time for the next phase of my extended journey down into Old Mexico.

Entropy in the Cobblestones: Living in San Miguel de Allende

DESPITE MY BAD sunburn and the onset of flu-like symptoms, I could only rest for a little while because Celia was due back in country the same day I returned to Mexico City myself. Carefully walking to avoid painful blue jean contact with the still sensitive, burned skin on my legs, I managed to grab a taxi in front of the Hotel Monte Carlo and met her on time at the airport.

Given my physical condition at the time, could I have been any luckier than to be waiting on a friend who happened to be a doctor? I don't think so. The first thing she did was take me to a *farmacia* where she bought some cream for my sunburn and some medicine for my flu symptoms. What a relief. What a break.

Naturally, I started feeling better right away. Not well, but better. After a couple of days in Mexico City during which time we visited the extraordinary Museum of Anthropology with its wonderful artifacts and miniature replica of ancient Tenochtitlan, the Aztec capital upon which Mexico City itself was built, we took a bus down to Cuernavaca. We needed to see some friends there and do a quick check on mail at Centro Bilingüe. In short order, we decided to head back north to spend some time in San Miguel de Allende.

San Miguel, in the state of Guanajuato, is a beautiful little mountain village with a well-established *gringo* artist colony. It is touristy but it has its charms, too, including a wonderful little *mercado,* cobblestone streets, and a lively nightlife. We split the rent on a local house for a month and set about familiarizing ourselves with the new surroundings. As so often happens when traveling about, we immediately ran into other friends from Cuernavaca and we formed a kind of running pack over the next few weeks.

Life for us temporary inhabitants of San Miguel was fun, entertaining, and exciting. For about a month, our inner circle lived the San Miguel life, learning Spanish and, in the case of some of our friends, studying at a local art school during the day and then partying most nights. I was still recovering from my sunburn-caused flu and my energy was somewhat down but I did my best to keep up.

What helped me finally get over my sunburn and flu, besides my personal doctor's care, was that I discovered the weekly *gringo* softball game on a dusty field down below and to the side of the town center. In my first game I had to run hard around the bases, and I believe the intense breathing broke the back of that long-lasting flu. From then on I got healthier and healthier. The weather in San Miguel, dry and sunny, reminded me of Arizona and that not only helped me feel better mentally and emotionally because of its familiarity but also because there's no better weather for beating a cold or flu.

Feeling better day by day did not inure me to an underlying negative aspect to life in San Miguel. Despite the town's charm and its active day and night life I discovered, slowly but steadily, that I had a problem with some of its people. Oh, not its native inhabitants, not the friendly locals, no it was the little *pueblo's* expatriate community, the more permanent *gringo* residents.

It wasn't that they were bad people or anything, although it seemed like some of them were perhaps peripherally involved in some shady dealings, it was that their lives there in San Miguel seemed to have no center, no base. This expatriate world felt entropic, like a black hole made of humans. It was a world in which you would be swallowed by the lack of moral certitude, by inaction, by the absence of any day-to-day purpose other than eating and drinking well and complaining about your lot in life.

This attitude wore on me greatly and when Celia left to go back to the states at the end of our month's lease and all of our other friends left within a few days of her, I found myself completely alone in San Miguel and not terribly happy about it. I moved into the Hotel San Sebastian where I spent a week or so in a directionless funk, drinking too much, and trying to figure out what my next move would be.

Before I came up with this plan, however, I did have one of the better epiphanies of my life, maybe the best, and it didn't concern me. It was instead a realization about the value and importance of my mother.

As I like to say, "if you're lucky enough, sometimes you live long enough to learn something." Luckily for me, both parts of that statement came true while I was sitting there alone in San Miguel de Allende, Guanajuato, Mexico, contemplating my future.

If You're Lucky Enough, Sometimes You Live Long Enough to Learn Something

THERE I WAS, then, sitting alone in my pleasant little room at the Hotel San Sebastian in San Miguel de Allende, up and across the street from the Academia Hispano language school. I was feeling lonesome and sorry for myself because all my friends had taken off during the last week. I was completely by myself.

So I began to contemplate a run down to Oaxaca to check the town out and also maybe go see the ruins at nearby Monte Alban. I had heard positive things about both places and thought I might make a little trip down south and see for myself. There was not much left for me to do in San Miguel, that was for sure.

I hadn't made a firm decision on that yet, though, and so I was sitting around my room, reading, writing, or making writing notes and kind of lightly wallowing in some old fashioned self-pity. I was sipping on a beer and sort of giving my life, as I had lived it up to that point, a shallow analysis.

Like most, if not all, youngest children in a family, the baby as it were, I grew up with an exaggerated sense of my own self-importance. Everything was done for me, everything was about me. I was the smartest, I was the hippest, I was the one who would be so successful.

While I was pondering these weighty topics and how wonderful I

Phydella Hogan 1974.
J. B. Hogan Collection

was, a funny thing happened. A light bulb went on. An idea formed in my mind. I had a little epiphany. I suddenly understood something. A concept I'd never come in contact with before was suddenly revealed to me in considerable clarity. I realized that I wasn't special at all. It wasn't that I was bad or anything, it's that maybe the "bright baby" hype was a tad overblown.

In place of my over-hyped self, I began to see clearly then that it wasn't me in my family who was special but someone else. And who was that someone else? Quite simply, it was my mother. She was the one who was special. She had raised four children by herself (my old man had bailed not long before my birth, making me born just "inside wedlock") with a country school eighth grade education. She had worked and sacrificed her entire young adulthood to make sure we were all fed, clothed, and housed, and she had done this in a time and place (the late 1940s and early 1950s in the South) where such a thing for a woman in her situation was practically impossible, at best.

And when she had nearly finished raising all of us, she took her first steps toward becoming a poet. She made herself a fine one, too. A lifelong musician, she was a whiz on the banjo and, driven by a desire to educate herself, she was a voracious reader. Poetry fit the bill perfectly for her creative impulse in language. She eventually had a couple of hundred poems published in small journals and put together a couple of books of her collected poetry.

Finally, in her late 60s and retired, she fulfilled a lifelong dream. She passed the GED (with the highest score the lady at the testing center had ever seen) and enrolled in college. She earned a bachelor's degree with honors from the University of Arkansas at the ripe old age of 74. Her later years were filled with some measure of deserved local celebrity and appreciation for the things she had accomplished against all odds.

Luckily for me I realized how special she was before her death and I tried to act accordingly over the last years of her life. I was going on forty-three years old when I had my realization about who the special person was in my family and I will be eternally grateful for that brief moment of insight that came to me in the pleasant little room in the Hotel San Sebastian in sleepy, dusty little San Miguel de Allende, Mexico.

It was proof positive, at least to me, that it is never, ever, too late to learn something about your life that will make it and you better. I got lucky in that hotel room. I will never forget it.

The Phillies Cap
from Ameca Ameca

WHENEVER I WAS in a *mercado* down in Mexico, I was, despite being a non-meat eater myself, always drawn to the butcher stalls. This was where you could see life as it used to be. Dead birds with unpicked feathers intact. Chunks of raw animal flesh lying out in the open with insects buzzing around. And my personal favorite, the heads of goats, staring you right in the face.

I would go back to the butcher area, mostly to force myself to face reality. I wanted to keep myself from becoming a complete weenie about the reality that probably 98 percent of the non-Hindu/Buddhist world, unlike myself, was still carnivorous and that in places like Mexico (and Kenya, as I had seen back in 1984) the open, unselfconscious buying and consumption of fresh meat was still a part of everyday life.

One of my favorite *mercados* was in the tiny *pueblo* of Ameca Ameca. Ameca Ameca sits beneath the awesome majesty of Ixtaccihuatl which, along with Popocatepetl, constitute the twin volcanoes (Ixta and Popo we *gringos* called them for short) of south central Mexico. The language school tour from Cuernavaca that I and my fellow students had signed up for first stopped at Popo where I made a brief, black-dusty, chilly hike toward the volcano base before lunch.

J.B. HOGAN

Afterward, we hopped on the tour bus and drove over to Ameca Ameca and its quaint little marketplace.

The vendors there sold the usual fare, *pulseras* (bracelets), cheap clothing, some Mexican knick knacks (Ameca Ameca didn't seem to be on the usual foreign tourist route so there were fewer souvenir items than most of the markets I'd visited in Mexico). However, I did find a cheap bag that I expected to use in future travels around the country and then as I was preparing to head over to the bus for the ride back to Cuernavaca, I spotted what I had been needing. A new baseball cap.

After checking out a few other caps, I chose a Philadelphia Phillies one as the best of the lot. Not because I was big on the Phillies, although I do follow them like any other baseball fan, but because it was a cool hat. I may have haggled a bit, not much, and I bought the cap for 2800 pesos. The exchange rate at the time was 2270 pesos to the dollar so it only cost about $1.25, a major bargain as far as I was concerned. From that day on, from Cuernavaca to Mexico City, Merida and the Yucatan and back, and on the return to San Miguel de Allende, if I was outside in the sun that Phillies hat was protecting my soon to be baldy-boy head.

As briefly alluded to before, in those days, the late spring of 1988, on Saturday afternoon (and the rare Sunday) there was a *gringo* slow pitch game at a little field a few blocks east of San Miguel's *jardín* (town square or garden). The field was all dirt, a little on the rough side but bearable, with no bases (we used cardboard in the time-honored fashion of pickup games) and no fences. The outfield was wide open in right and center field but down the left field line was a tall tree outside the assumed foul line and some sort of ditch that served as a natural and not terribly deep left field barrier. A solid punch down the line would usually get you a homerun, as the outfielder had to avoid crashing into the ditch and then also retrieve the ball from among the dusty rocks and scrub grass behind.

The local *gringos* were somewhat slow to accept a newcomer like me into their midst and so it took me a couple of games before my play started getting me noticed. Soon I was among the first picked in the choosing up of teams before each Saturday's game. We usually played two games during the afternoon and as I recall, the games tended to last until everybody felt it was finally time to call it a day. When we had had enough softball, we split back to our homes, apartments, or rooms to get ready for the night's carousing in San Miguel's lively bar scene.

One game day, not long before I left San Miguel for the fact-finding trip to Oaxaca and another stop in Ameca Ameca, I secured my status as a top player among the other permanent and temporary expatriates. We had been playing several innings that hot, dry Saturday when the guy in front of me hit a bomb of a homerun, a grand slam no less, to clear the bases and give us a big lead.

Then, when the excitement had settled down, I stepped in as the next hitter, bases empty. Remarkably, for I was never a power hitter, I also drove a shot down the line in left and it, too, cleared the left fielder and beyond him into that ditch and I hustled around the bases for a solo homerun. Two in a row, consecutive homeruns. For some reason, my solo shot seemed to impress my team more than the kid's grand slam and the next Saturday I was the first player chosen.

BY THE FIRST week of May, you will recall, all my San Miguel friends took off for the U.S. within a matter of days. The place cleared out. Left alone, I decided to head down to Oaxaca to see what it was like there. I took a first class bus from the south station (Cristóbal Colón) in Mexico City, made the second, brief stop in Ameca Ameca, then traveled on to Oaxaca and farther points south.

Oaxaca itself was an excellent experience. I found a little language school there, roamed casually around its sub-tropically green streets, and visited the amazing, awesome ruins of Monte Alban. Monte Alban sits atop a large mountain with a spectacular, 360-degree view of the tree and farm-dotted valleys surrounding the ancient, long-dead civilization. I also made an entertaining side trip down to the neat little coastal town of Puerto Escondido, where I ran into friends from not only San Miguel but also one from earlier school days in Cuernavaca.

After my trip to the south, I returned to San Miguel to pick up my few belongings (I'd left them at the Hotel San Sebastian) in anticipation of shifting my base of operations down to Oaxaca. I made it back to San Miguel in time for one last Saturday softball game.

At the San Miguel ballfield, I found almost all the same *gringos* still there. One of the things about San Miguel was that its expatriate community, outsiders as they were in the tiny hill community, did tend to hang together, both for their good and their detriment. Anyway, it was the same old gang and they greeted me as if I had not even been gone. Sporting my Phillies cap, I joined the circle of players for the ritual choosing of sides. One of the guys, who was always a team captain, checked over the group and with no hesitation took me first.

"Phillies hat. You're on mine."

That fast, that easily, he remembered me as "Phillies hat," the good ballplayer. Recalling that makes me smile. At forty-two, going on forty-three, it made me feel that even though it was only a little pickup game in the middle of nowhere Mexico, I was still skilled enough to be chosen first. It was also a kick to see that my choice of caps from the quaint little market in Ameca Ameca had been the right one. I was "Phillies hat." The other *gringos* might not have ever learned my actual name but they knew I could play ball and they would remember me by my cap.

That afternoon was the last time I ever played ball in San Miguel, even though I would spend time there again in 1989 and in

1992. We played two games that afternoon. I was selected first for the second tilt, too, and I happily zoomed around the dirt field in my Phillies cap beneath the hot Mexican sky. I had an excellent last day, making one good, long running catch in the outfield and going three for six at the plate.

I enjoyed those last ball games on the dusty fields of San Miguel de Allende. They were like a last, brief flash of my youth, absorbed forever into the clinging amber of persistent memory. I still have the Phillies cap to this day. It's folded up, top of the hat over and under the bill, like we used to do in old baseball days, and stored in a keep-sake box. I keep it to remind myself of the fun I had down in San Miguel. I don't ever plan to get rid of it.

"Los Bases Estan Llenos, Como El Freeway: Bumper a Bumper"

ON MY SOUTHERN trip before that last visit to San Miguel, I was so impressed with the grandeur of Monte Alban and the sub-tropical beauty of Oaxaca that I decided I should look into living there a while. Luckily, near the *jardín,* the standard Mexican city *zocalo* or town square, I found a little language school. It was run by two wonderful younger women and I hit it off with them right away. They offered to get me an apartment in a building right behind their school, and that was all the encouragement I needed.

I flew back to Mexico City and hopped a bus to San Miguel to pick up my belongings at the San Sebastian. I stayed a couple of days in San Miguel, playing those final softball games, and then headed back to Oaxaca. On the way down, I passed through Ameca Ameca again where I had purchased my near and dear Phillies hat.

Things went as planned in Oaxaca. The ladies helped me get an apartment in back of the school. I was subletting it while the usual tenant, another U.S. guy, was traipsing around Mexico buying indigenous toys and dolls to sell and make some sort of living with. I settled into my new place right away and began taking classes in Spanish and Mexican history and culture at the little school.

Oaxaca was lushly green and pleasant most of the time, and its *jardín* life was the place to get a bite to eat or a beer, or to simply watch people. At my apartment I set up shop, bought groceries, beer, and other items to make it my own space for at least a few weeks.

One of my favorite things to do in the apartment, especially in the evenings, was to listen to Los Angeles Dodgers baseball in Spanish. The Dodgers network was beamed all over Mexico, and other countries in the region as well I'm sure. They had two announcers, René Cardenas and Jaime Jarrín. I liked both announcers a lot and enjoyed their broadcasts. I learned some Spanish language versions of baseball announcer talk from these gentlemen.

I remember the following phrase clearly. *"Le tira… y se poncha!"* Which in English is probably the equivalent to "Here's the pitch… he struck him out!" Another one was *"Se va, se va, se fue!"* This is a fun one because it's the Spanish version of Harry Caray's old home run call. "It might be, it could be, it is!" More precisely, it means, "going, going, gone." But my favorite phrase, and I think it was Jaime Jarrín's, was *"Los bases estan llenos como el Freeway, boomper a boomper."* The translation, "The bases are full like the freeway, bumper to bumper." What fun announcers.

I ended up spending six weeks in Oaxaca, becoming good friends with the women who ran the school. We enjoyed museums and art shows together, visited a giant tree outside the city that would tell you when you were going to die if you hugged it (being superstitious I declined this experience), and they took me to banks and travel agents to get me squared away for my eventual return trip to Mexico City and the U.S.

At about the end of my time in Oaxaca, the Mexican presidential race was heating up. Carlos Salinas de Gortari, or Calvito (Baldy Boy), was the candidate for PRI, the long-standing primary political party in the country, and therefore the assumed victor in the upcoming elections.

This year, 1988, however, was proving to be a rather hotly, and unexpectedly, contested race because of the popularity of a left-center coalition candidate by the name of Cuauhtémoc Cardenas, the son of Mexico's most popular president of the twentieth century Lazaro Cardenas. I was going back to Mexico City so that I would be there and see the elections up close and personal.

After those six enjoyable weeks in Oaxaca, I caught the slow, overnight train to Mexico City. Catching a taxi at the train station, I was soon ensconced at the Hotel Monte Carlo, my home away from home in the big city.

Staying in
D. H. Lawrence's House

BACK IN SPRING while we were studying together in Cuernavaca, Tomas my Norwegian friend first turned me onto the Hotel Monte Carlo, located about three blocks from Mexico City's enormous *zocalo* or central plaza. The Monte Carlo, not particularly impressive from without, was at 69 Calle Uruguay, and was a favorite of the young European traveling set. Italians, French, Spanish, Scandinavians, and a small cadre of usually well-traveled Americans stayed there as well.

The Monte Carlo offered clean, well-kept single and double rooms with or without baths (there were public showers on two levels as I recall). The going rate in 1988 for a room without bath was right at $6 a night, which was outstanding, even at that time. They had a single room on the roof of the building, too. I stayed there one time when the rest of the hotel was completely booked up. It was a pretty special place to stay, being up on the roof by itself and all.

Besides being safe and comfortable, the Monte Carlo had facilities, like most hotels in Mexico, for storing travelers' belongings while they gallivanted around the country, and a helpful and amiable staff. Across from the main desk was a small area with a large television and three or four rows of chairs and maybe a couch for watching programs and chatting with your new-found friends from far flung places. All in all, it was a charming and inexpensive place to stay and whenever I was in Mexico after my first trip to Cuernavaca, I always stayed at the Monte Carlo.

The hotel's other claim to fame, besides some clearly visible cracks from the terrible earthquake that hit Mexico City in the late 70s or early 80s, was that it had once been the British writer D. H. Lawrence's home. The entire hotel. Lawrence used it as his home base when he traveled to North America, also spending time in the American desert southwest, for his health.

I believe he was dying of consumption and his doctors had prescribed the dry, warm air of Mexico and the United States as a means of combatting his illness. In 1988, when I first started staying at the Monte Carlo, I didn't yet know about the D. H. Lawrence connection, but the hotel certainly left me with some vivid traveling memories.

So, after my sojourn in Oaxaca, I returned to the Monte Carlo and settled in for a few days before my return to the U.S. For one thing, I wanted to see how the elections would turn out. I'd never seen an election in a foreign country before (not counting ones I might have missed in Japan and Korea in the service) and this one, with Cardenas apparently getting more popular daily, promised to be exciting. The buzz was that he might defeat Salinas de Gortari and the PRI political machine.

During the last couple of days before the election I asked everyone I could in Mexico City who they were going to vote for. The response was one hundred percent in favor of Cardenas. Now, that would be something. PRI unseated after sixty-five years in power, and by a leftist-coalition candidate. It's true Cardenas had moved more to the center toward the end of the campaign, but he was clearly a socialist, and he had his daddy's name.

The father, Lazaro Cardenas, had been so bold as to nationalize the oil industry and the country's banks back in the 1930s. The elder Cardenas has been practically deified for his extreme populist (in the good, original sense of that word) stance and his openness to the people (he refused bodyguards and would have interviews and meetings with people off the street). He was not only Mexico's favorite *presidente* since Benito Juarez, he was mine as well and now his son had, apparently, a real shot at shaking up the Mexican power structure once again. It was an exciting prospect.

While waiting for the elections, by chance I met a young woman named Tali from Israel down in the TV room at the Monte Carlo. She was open and friendly and, amazingly enough, friends with Billy, my old Missouri pal from Peru, who had recently gone down to Nicaragua to work for the revolution.

My new acquaintance and I quickly became fast friends and went around Mexico City together, visiting the government building on the *zocalo*. This building not only houses several murals by Diego Rivera but also provides the little balcony where *El Presidente,* whoever he may be, yells out his *"grito"* (cry) of independence on September 15 at midnight.

Later, we hit the marketplaces, especially the artisan ones, to pick up trinkets to take back to our respective native countries. I bought bunches of cheap little things for my family and friends as mementos of my trip. You know, the sort of "He went to Mexico and all I got was this crappy cheap whatever" that you see on T-shirts people bring back from Cancun and the like.

One morning while Tali and I were chatting, we discovered we had another friend in common, Ben, a Tecnica volunteer who had helped me down in Nicaragua the year before. Remarkably, he happened to be in Mexico City right then and so we called him and set up a get together for the next morning, election day.

Election day dawned bright and clear and the three of us had a great time together. We ate pizza in a little café, where they both chided me for tipping the waiter like a local (that is, not much), went around to many of the shops on the streets leading away from the *zocalo,* and walked by the reconstructed ruins of Tenochtitlan, the Aztec capital, upon which the Spaniards built Mexico City.

We eventually ended up on the roof of the Latin American Tower, with its I don't know how many floors above the sinking ground of the *gran ciudad,* and then had a small meal at Sanborn's House of Tiles, an affordable restaurant only a few blocks up from the *zocalo.* Afterward, we went by several voting locations to see how things were going and simply enjoyed ourselves in general until Ben had to excuse himself and head back to his home there in the city.

The next morning Tali and I ate breakfast together, said our good-byes, and then I saw her off in a taxi headed for the airport. I stopped by a local bookstore to pick up some Spanish/English picture dictionaries as gifts and then it was time for me to leave as well. I grabbed a taxi, too, and was at the airport in plenty of time to catch my Delta flight from Mexico City to Los Angeles and on to Tucson.

While waiting for my flight, I checked the local papers and saw that, despite an apparent landslide for Cardenas in the Distrito Federal (Federal District, of which gigantic Mexico City is a part), Salinas de Gortari had been declared the new president of Mexico by a margin of something like sixty to forty percent. There were immediate cries of vote tampering, especially in the D. F., but Salinas de Gortari was the president, PRI had won again, as expected. History had not been made. Not this time.

On the way home my flight had to maneuver in and around large storm clouds over northern Mexico, but all went well and after a short layover in Los Angeles, I arrived back in Tucson around ten fifty-five at night. My long trip to Mexico, entertaining and enlightening as it had been, was over.

You Can Never
Repeat the Past

I MADE THREE trips to Mexico between 1988 and 1992. The first, already described, was five months long. The second, for two months, was at the end of 1989, and the last one, also for two months, came in the summer of 1992.

The 1989 trip was terribly anti-climactic after the intensity and depth of the long one in 1988. But a couple of things happened that I recall.

I managed to make one new friend, a chef from Denver. He taught me the following truism. If you're going to drink and drive, be sure to take a car. He was a funny guy and he always called me Kenny Rogers because at that stage of my life I apparently looked like "The Gambler."

Also on that trip, at its beginning, as I was coming into Mazatlán I saw the giant Cervecería Pacifico (Pacifico Brewery) to the east of the railroad tracks. Once in Mazatlán I checked into the Hotel Villa Del Mar in old town Mazatlán and went out to get a bite to eat and hopefully a bottle of Pacifico.

"Algo para tomar, señor?" The waiter at the restaurant asked me. "Something to drink, sir?"

"Una cerveza Pacifico, por favor."

"Lo siento, señor, no hay Pacifico. I'm sorry, sir, there isn't any Pacifico."

Huh? What? No Pacifico? I had just seen the brewery when I came into town. How could this be possible? The first place I try doesn't carry the hometown beer? Are you kidding me?

It was, apparently, the only restaurant in the entire city of Mazatlán, old town and new, that did not serve Pacifico. What the heck? Since that time, however, I have managed to consume a fair amount of Pacifico—it's one of my favorite brews. But at that restaurant a couple of miles from the brewery there was no doing. Odd, weird, and funny all at once.

The other thing I remember from this trip were all the people who seemed to think I was country singer Kenny Rogers. I had more hair then, and it was white, and I had a white beard. I guess that was enough. Several times people asked me if I was Rogers or they simply greeted me with "Hey, Kenny Rogers."

This Kenny Rogers phase had started a few years back with a couple of cute little Okie kids in Tucson. They lived at the first apartment complex where I did after I was on my own again. To get your mail at these apartments, you had to pass through the pool area to get to the mailboxes. One day after work as I was navigating this course, a little boy called out to me.

"Hey, you." He was brash and had a heavy country accent. His little sister hung by his side. "You, Kenny Rogers."

"What?" I laughed.

"You, you're Kenny Rogers."

"Wish I was. I'd be rich."

"Hey, you, Kenny Rogers." The little sister had that same Okie accent. "Sing us a country western song."

Well, that cracked me up big time. After that, when I saw those little kids, we'd go through the same routine. It tickled me no end. And oddly enough, it seemed to catch on all over the place. People on the streets would ask me if I was Kenny. My pals made fun of me and called me Kenny.

I'm sure it would have been a terrible insult to the real Kenny Rogers, but it was funny to me there in Tucson.

Then it followed me to Mexico. Several people on the streets called me that or asked me if I was Kenny. And even back at Centro Bilingüe, where I went to study again, people pointed out my similarity to the music star.

And the chef buddy that I met in San Miguel de Allende (yes, I went back to visit this old haunt as well on this second trip south of the border) thought I looked so much like Rogers that he just called me Kenny all the time. Later, back in Tucson, others would continue to mistake me for the singer. Finally, luckily, fortunately, in a few years my hair began to fall out and the Kenny Rogers stream of mistaken identity moments trickled down to a dry creek bed of nothing. By then I didn't miss those little moments, anyway.

With some pride, however, I noticed that if I let my beard and hair (what remained of it) grow as long as I could, I did bear some resemblance to Karl Marx. In keeping with the new look, I cultivated a Marxist attitude. I spoke of historical imperatives, of equal pay for equal work, of surplus value. Oh, yeah, I was cool now. Well, maybe not so much! You can imagine a Marxist routine didn't do much for a guy in corporate-dominated America in the latter years of the twentieth century.

Anyway, I ended the 1989 trip with a journey to San Blas, a tiny beach town below Mazatlán. I took the overnight train from Mexico City to Guadalajara and then on to Tepic. Most of the second part of that trip I sat beside an attractive woman named Luz Maria who I will never forget. Not only was she pretty but she somehow made me feel as if we were traveling together as a couple. She was cool.

From Tepic, I took a bus out to San Blas, riding in one of those classic chickens in the aisle, passengers piled to the roof, type *Segunda Clase* (second-class) buses that you read about and see in silly movies. On the way to San Blas I spoke briefly with some Mexican cowboys and their families and felt unique as I was the only *gringo* not only on the bus to San Blas but even in the Tepic station, as well.

San Blas's main claim to fame is its jungle boat excursion down a muddy river to a banana plantation where you can have a meal and some beer at the end of your exciting ride. On the way back, I spotted the only crocodile we saw, a point of pride to me. In the little *zocalo* or central plaza in San Blas, I saw the cowboys again and we exchanged friendly nods and single finger (not that finger!) salutes to the hat in what I took to be a display of mutual respect. It was one of the highlights of the trip for me.

Two days later, I caught the train back up to Mazatlán, spent another day or two there, and then headed back to Nogales, Sonora and Nogales, Arizona. From the U.S. side I took a bus to Tucson where I would shortly begin a technical writing contract with IBM.

I arrived in Tucson at a most unusual time, right in the middle of a snowstorm. I called my friend David to give me a lift to a motel, and I stayed there until the paperwork for my contract cleared whatever hurdles it had to clear. I was back in the states, again, and I was back at work, again. As my Tucson buddy Manny would say, "same-o same-o."

Well, You Can *Almost* Repeat the Past—Sometimes

I MADE MY third and last trip down into Mexico (later trips to the border at Nogales do not count) in 1992. This time I decided to spend all of my time, with the exception of necessary travel connections in Mexico City, in San Miguel de Allende. I had tried to reproduce my 1988 Cuernavaca experience again in 1989 and that had not gone well. This would be my third time in San Miguel, but maybe that would be the charm. As it turned out, it might not have been the charm, but it was a darned good time.

Luckily, I made friends right away with Dana, a young teacher from Bartlesville, Oklahoma, and she was my introduction into the social world of our language school, Academia Hispano. There was a large group of students of various ages from Bartlesville besides Dana and also a smaller, but highly entertaining, group from Austria. At first, I hung mostly with the Bartlesville crowd but midway through my time in San Miguel I shifted over, excepting Dana, to the *Austriacos* (Austrians in Spanish).

I did so for a simple reason: a twenty-one year old, blonde girl, named Suzie. How I ended up spending time with this lovely young Austrian girl still eludes me fully, but we were in a Mexican Literature class together at the Academia, and we flirted a lot between lessons on B. Traven (much of which I presented to the class myself).

Then one night at Pancho y Lefty's, the same bar I had frequented in '88 and '89, I was half-drunk and dancing with one of the Bartlesville girls when suddenly Suzie shows up and wants to dance with me. In short order we are dancing exclusively with one another and began hanging out together outside language school and the bars.

I did everything I knew to advance my position with Suzie, but it never got past the flirting, pecks on the cheek, dancing to rock and roll with reckless abandon phase. I guess I was a little too old for her. To this day, I wouldn't trade one second of the time I got to be with her. No man in his right mind would.

Besides the partying in Pancho y Lefty's, I used to go with my rotating and moveable sets of friends, the Okies and the Austrians, to several other bars in San Miguel including the tequila bar El Ring, where in '88 I had my knife confiscated while I was in the club thereby making me feel like a real outlaw of some kind. The other bar was La Taberna del Rey, a small bar on the second floor of a building up the street from El Ring, closer to the jardín.

La Taberna had a young rock band who did a mean version of Nirvana's "Smells Like Teen Spirit" and we, that is, Dana and a few more of the Bartlesville folks and me, became fans and then friends with the guys in the band. Each time we went out, which was most nights, we would check to see if the band, the lead guitar player and singer was a young guy from Athens, Georgia named David, was playing at La Taberna or not. Most times they were and we partied regularly to their music.

In those days, there was an excellent restaurant in San Miguel called Casa Mexas which was owned by a young couple from Texas. In 1988 the restaurant had been a little place on an out of the way street above the *jardín,* but in '89 they'd moved below town center and in '92 had expanded to include a large dining area, a back room with pool tables, and a TV room as well. It was a place to hang when I wanted to do something other than sit in my apartment reading

J. B. "The Gambler" Hogan, Gusano Rojo worm on tongue, San Miguel de Allende,
Guanajuato, Mexico, 1992.
J. B. Hogan Collection

Don Quixote (which was a wonderful experience by the way) and drinking wine by myself.

Sometimes I would meet some new friends in town, including a couple who also lived in Tucson, although I didn't know them there. We celebrated the very attractive woman's birthday in a small, out of the way, restaurant favored by hip locals and sharp visitors.

Another fine woman I knew on this trip was a lovely Japanese woman, Yasuko, who was preparing to study at a large university in Mexico City. She was the antithesis of the stereotypes we are taught about Japanese women. Independent and liberated, she was studying abroad while her husband remained in Japan. She was of indeterminate age, maybe mid- to late forties, but she had a sweet smile that made her look like she was more like twenty-five years old, it was remarkable.

Because my Japanese friend did not know English, one of the interesting aspects of our relationship was that we had to speak in Spanish to communicate with one another. During our time together at the Academia Hispano in San Miguel, Yasuko and I did quite a few things together, dancing at the disco tequila bar El Ring, visiting the local Museum of Fine Arts, studying together, and on one memorable afternoon being treated to a taste testing of all the truly fine brands of tequila by a well off and generous expatriate Yankee retiree.

The last big event of my time in San Miguel on this trip was a party I attended given by all my young Austrian friends. Because they knew I was a vegetarian, they played a trick on me with a bottle of Gusano Rojo *mescal.* That's right, Red Worm *mescal,* the one with the little booze-soaked dead worm at the bottom of the bottle.

My *Austriaco* pals worked the last drink of the bottle down to where only I could get it and, therefore, the worm. They were all grinning as I finished off the bottle. Playing along with the gag, I allowed the worm to enter my mouth and then stuck it alongside my jaw teeth where I kept it safely while ingesting the last of the *mescal.* Finally, after letting the drama build, I opened my mouth wide and stuck out my tongue with the little dead worm resting right on the tip.

The *Austriacos,* young men and women, cried out with joy at my subterfuge. Laughing aloud myself, I dropped the little worm onto the floor, but it was quickly retrieved and cleaned off so that I could re-enact the moment for a camera someone produced. I still have that photo and looking at it always brings back fond memories of the last big falling-off-the -wagon phase in my life and of the young Austrian friends who cheered me on in these last rambunctious party days.

Next morning I prepared to pull out of San Miguel for Mexico City and then back home. As I walked down the hill away from town toward the bus station, someone yelled at me. It was David, the lead singer of our favorite band from La Taberna del Rey. He called me over to say goodbye, and I will always appreciate that young man's courtesy in doing such a thing. I hope he made it in the music business or whatever field he ended up choosing. His kindness in showing respect like that to an old guy stands out still in my memory. It was a cool way to leave town.

After a week or so in Mexico City, during which time I did little except visit the Leon Trotsky Museum over in Coyoacan (the nearby Frida Kahlo museum was closed during this time), I hopped a first class bus to Nuevo Laredo. The most memorable part of the return trip was stopping at a bus station restaurant in San Luis Potosi about eleven o'clock at night where I was literally the only *gringo* in sight. It felt cool to be such at that time and I was completely comfortable with it. Early the next day I crossed the bridge into Laredo, Texas and my last big trip to Mexico was complete.

Now, this third and final trip to Mexico may not have gone as well as the one in 1988, proving that you might not be able to exactly go home again, but it was an excellent experience on its own. Considering how special 1988 had been, I had to admit that wasn't half bad. No sir, not half bad at all.

Focusing on
the End Game

AFTER THE 1992 trip to Mexico, I made a conscious decision to shift my emphasis from traveling south of the border to hanging out in the American south with my mother as she moved into her later years. It was the right choice.

My mother was remarkable for a number of reasons. Now any decent mom is remarkable in and of herself, how can a person ask for anything better, but our mother did some things and had some qualities that I believe raise her up even above your normal, wonderful mom.

First of all, she raised four kids by herself with not a lot of help and only an eighth grade education and little or no work experience. At least not much when our old man and she broke up and she was forced to enter the work force to care for all of us right after my birth in 1945.

In order to feed and clothe us all, she worked cleaning other people's houses, she took in washing and ironing, and she labored at a local garment factory (what is now referred to as a sweatshop). Finally, she settled in, for many years, as a restaurant worker. As a cook, waitress, and manager.

In addition to obviously being a hard worker, she was a highly intelligent person whose natural inclination toward schooling had been cut off by the limitations and harsher realities of the age in which she had been brought up. Rather than stunt her however, those limitations instilled in her a fierce desire for knowledge and education, and she in turn instilled those values into all of us kids, and most definitely into me.

She read voraciously, if not always discriminatingly, and my earliest memories are of her reading to me, patiently, repeatedly, and teaching me how to read on my own. There is no way to quantify or qualify the value of that reading. No one could ask for more of a parent than that alone.

She was also a gifted musician, and before a goiter operation ruined her voice, a fine singer, as well. Raised in a family of musical siblings, she was almost a virtuoso on the banjo and could play guitar and bass and other instruments, too. Her brothers and sisters were excellent musicians themselves, and the family's musical story, especially that of my mother and her sister, my Aunt Helen, is given in a fine work by University of Arkansas professor Robert Cochran entitled *Singing in Zion.* The book was completed but not quite published shortly before my mother's death. She did see the galleys of the book but not the final product.

About 1960, my mother took up writing poetry at the instigation of my Aunt Bill (her real name was Alma but she got the nickname Billie because she was a tomboy as a girl) who is also featured in *Singing in Zion.* Aunt Bill wrote some fine poetry herself, and she prompted her little sister, my mother, into pursuing the muse. Over the years, as I commented elsewhere, my mother published innumerable poems in small literary journals and put out two or three collections of her work.

Our mother was also a practical person. She taught each of us boys how to take care of ourselves by showing us how to sew buttons on shirts and darn holes in socks, how to iron clothes, and how to cook. All three of us made considerable use of these small skills during our separate times in the U.S. Air Force, and also when we found ourselves single, which has happened from time to time, hard though this may be for you to believe. Ha, ha.

She also had a real knack for manipulating whatever job she had in order to benefit us kids. When she was at restaurants we managed to get fed regularly on the cheap, and when she worked as a book-keeper at a clothing store in Lincoln, Nebraska, she kept me and my brother and his brood of kids in coats, shoes and boots for ridiculously low prices. She always had some kind of edge that allowed us to get what we needed at a price we could afford. No small skill that.

When my mother finally retired in the mid-1980s, she decided she would take a long-delayed crack at higher education by attending the University of Arkansas. To get into the university she had to pass a GED test. And pass it she did. As I mentioned previously, the lady at the testing center said it was the highest score she had ever seen. That was all it took, my mother was back in school after a mere fifty year gap.

As befits a family steeped in literature, my mother majored in English (like me and my sister Martha, as well), and she spent the next several years inspiring other students and her professors, too, graduating with honors in 1992 at the age of 74. We held several parties for her that summer, and all her kids and most of their kids came to town to celebrate with the new college graduate.

Although she had another four years of independent living before she began declining in health, my mother didn't quite have the energy to pursue a Master's degree, even though the school had already offered her scholarships and a teaching assistant position. When she got sick in 1996, leading to her final decline, I couldn't help but think what her life might have been like if she had been allowed to develop her intellectual nature. I'm sure that in another time she would have been a teacher, probably of younger students, and she would've been a good one.

Nonetheless, the latter years of her life were marked by late arriving respect from many quarters. She became something of a local, minor celebrity and people flocked to see her, making pilgrimages, as it were, to visit her before she passed. When she did die, in 1999, she was mourned and missed. All of us loved her, and her loss left a hole that nothing can, or ever will, fill. But that's to be expected when you lose someone who matters in life. And our mother mattered in life. Not only to the family but also to many other people as well. She was a special person, and special people are impossible to replace. You will always miss them. Always.

Y2K

IT TOOK ME about six months to get myself straightened out after my mother's death. Finally, toward the end of 1999, I landed a technical writing contract in Boulder and headed up there to work and live once more. I settled into my new apartment near the end of the year, in time to experience the madness of Y2K. Remember all that over-hyped silliness? I sure do.

If anything was ever overrated in my life, it had to be Y2K. The world was going to end on New Year's Eve 1999. And if that didn't happen, all of the computers on the planet would crash the next day, causing planes to fall indiscriminately out of the sky. With the Apocalypse at hand, I also assumed that Jesus would be coming shortly to round up all us sinners and probably get himself a cheap Hummer to drive to the final meeting of the local Republican Party.

I was so thrilled with the semi-panic that semi-gripped the public that about eleven-thirty on New Year's Eve 1999 I went to a local supermarket to see what was going on. I had seen empty grocery stores in poverty-stricken Nicaragua in the 1980s and tornado-freaked out Sapulpa, Oklahoma in the 1990s, among other places, and so I wanted to see how Y2K matched up to those situations.

I was disappointed. The store I went to had been stripped of most of its goods all right. There was no bottled water left. But the place had not been cleaned out like I was expecting. There were still some icing mixes, crappy candy, and seasonal items left. A real end of the world scenario should have caused the place to be picked as clean as a wildebeest carcass on the plains of the Serengeti. At least that's what I kind of had in mind.

The truth was that Y2K didn't mean or change jack. For several years in advance, most big companies had been preparing for it and so there were no terrible computer glitches. No planes fell out of the sky either and Jesus didn't come back. Which is good or bad depending upon your religious point of view or lack thereof.

When it was all over, the change to the new millennium (which technically didn't occur until one year later) was exactly what it should have been, the arbitrary changing over of one arbitrary time frame to another. That's all it was and all that sort of thing will ever be. If the deconstructionists have ever had a point about the words, names, and concepts of our world being without objective meaning, Y2K would have to be it.

It did, however, provide a heck of a lot of people with an easy and cheap excuse to party like it was 1999 (pardon the oblique reference to Prince), which it was. And a fun party is not something you want to turn your nose up at. Especially when you're an old guy trying to keep from feeling like you are running out your own arbitrary string. When you get to be this old, you're even happy to be invited to a GI party for crying out loud!

AFTER THE Y2K nonsense, I realized that I needed to make some money to tide me over between a presumed end of my contracting career (there was no specific knowledge about the end of my contracting, only some barely formed notion of economic self-protection) and when I would be able or want to begin Social Security. Assuming no idiots in Washington, D.C. managed to wipe the program out.

So I made myself get to work, shut up about it, stop feeling sorry for myself (no self-pity, no complaining), and do the jobs I was assigned. Make the decent money, save as much as possible, prepare for life after contracting.

And that is basically what I did for the next three years, with one break while I fought with contract companies over my salary. A battle I won, by the way, a small victory but a victory nonetheless. When you work like that, there's not much to tell about. Endless work weeks, waiting for hump day, waiting for Friday, weekends that fly by, blah, blah, blah. Everyone who's ever worked knows the routine.

The only thing new I did was begin playing the upright and electric bass guitars and begin to get another couple of writing publications. I tried to enjoy my time with friends as much as possible and keep working on the music and the writing.

However, as year blended into year in the new millennium, I could tell my resolution to shut up and work was beginning to falter. Not an altogether unexpected situation, given my lack of penchant for working in the heart of one of America's largest and most monolithic mega-corporations. Soon that original Y2K resolution was forgotten.

Okay, That's Enough
of This Crap

TOWARD THE END of 2002 my shut-up-and-work campaign was out of steam. I had completely had it being a technical writer in Boulder, or anywhere else. I was annoyed with my working assignments, most of my technical contacts, upper management, blah, blah, blah.

I didn't even go back to work after the beginning of the new year until my lead writer called to ask me what it was exactly that I was doing. My lead writer, Janet, is a friend of mine and even with her patience and kindness to me, I was still mad as heck and I wasn't going to take it anymore. I managed to hang on until early April 2003 and then I quit my contract. I was done, finito, history. It was the last contract I would have and that was all she wrote.

About the middle of the month I took off in my six-year old Jeep and headed out of Colorado on a trip to see my Tucson friends and have a mini-reunion with some of my old Misawa buddies from Air Force days. Along the way I visited Billy the Kid's grave in New Mexico, spent the night in alien-obsessed Roswell, toured Carlsbad Caverns, and then drove all the way to El Paso on what was left of a tank of gas, pulling into the suburbs of that formerly little west Texas town with the needle hard into the empty range. That was a close call.

I spent the night at a motel in Las Cruces (or Las Crunches as I like to call it, for no logical reason) and then the next morning headed off to Tucson. I had the mini-reunion with my old service buds, afterward flying to San Diego for a visit with my long-time Missouri pal Perk and his wife CJ, with a side trip to the Imperial Valley to see my cousin Lloyd. On my way back to Colorado, I visited the Petrified Forest, the Painted Desert, and the cliff cities of Mesa Verde. Excellent stuff.

For the next year, I traveled, played some bass guitar in Nebraska and Iowa with my brother and our friends Bill and Jeanette (we were known collectively as Willow Creek), and spent most of my settled time in Ft. Collins, Colorado, one of my favorite places (I'm certainly not alone in that opinion).

Finally, I had the painful realization that without a well-paying job I couldn't afford to live in Colorado and so I decided to go back to Arkansas, my original home, where the cost of living is a lot less than it is in such places as Colorado and the desert southwest. In 2004, that's exactly what I did.

The Three R's—Readin', Researchin', and Ritin'

A FTER FORTY YEARS away, then, I moved back to my original hometown of Fayetteville, Arkansas. There had been so much growth here, especially over the previous ten to fifteen years, that the place was barely recognizable to me as the same town I grew up in. But it was inexpensive to live in and if I worked at it I could still find dozens, even hundreds, of memories by going around to certain streets that still looked a little like the old days.

The only places left in town where my family had lived were the apartments on South Street that my mother and I and my middle brother Joe lived in right before he went into the Air Force back in 1958; the house on Duncan Street that my mother and I lived in when I was a member of the not so fearsome Duncan Street Tarantulas (my childhood pals Jim, Roy, and Ron) and; most poignantly, 812 York (now Cleveland) Street where my grandfather, Dad Gilbert, died.

Times are different now, though. Dad has been gone some seventy years, and the old town is not the same as it used to be. Of course, neither am I. What I am now, however, is a writer, making almost no money, of course, and a local historian. Back home after so many years away I discovered two things. A strong interest in local history before 1961 when I moved away and especially during the Great Depression—and the existence of online literary journals.

Discovering Internet Publishing

WOW, JUST WOW. The explosion of online literary journals that I discovered in 2004-2005 was an absolute miracle to me and gave me the outlet for my writing that I'd been seeking for twenty-five years. At that point, I had two publications, both in print journals, to show for a quarter century of trying.

But thanks to the proliferation of online journals and receptive editors, my publications total went from 2 short stories in 2003, to 247 at the end of 2013. Two publications the first 25 years, 245 in the next ten (145 poems and 100 stories).

At first, I thought I should try to get each separate poem or story published in a different journal, but I soon found that certain editors seemed to favor my work so I would repeat with them. Even so, there were still lots of rejections, even from journals where I had multiple publications. I have a good-sized folder of acceptances that I keep but I have a much larger one of rejections—that's the reality of writing.

Some of the early journals that published my work, mostly now defunct, were *Megaera, The Square Table* (out of New York), *The Copperfield Review, Bewildering Stories* (sci-fi and such), and *Poesia*—a local print journal run then by my friend, local poet, and lawyer Bill Mayo.

J. B. Hogan and Kirby L. Estes, Poetry Reading, Fayetteville, Arkansas, 2007. Photo by Martha Hogan Estes

To date, my scribblings (fictional and otherwise) have resulted in the publication (mostly online) of over 350 poems and stories. The natural progression from here, of course, would be getting books published and I'll get to that a little bit later.

Local History Boy

B ESIDES GIVING ME the opportunity to focus on writing poetry and stories, my return home also expanded my interest in local history (I had already spent a few years researching local minor league baseball history for my book *Angels in the Ozarks*). So I began to spend much of my time with what I like to call, and mentioned earlier, the Three R's: Readin', Researchin', and Ritin'.

The research and writing of local history led me to places I never thought I'd be. I joined the Washington County Historical Society and ended up serving two consecutive one-year terms as its president. I became a member of the Fayetteville Historic District Commission and served one year as its chair. And I was offered and accepted a position on the board of the Historic Cane Hill organization, which is a remarkable project with the goal of restoring this charming, historic little western Washington County town.

Over the years, I have also taught many local history classes for the University of Arkansas Continuing Education's Osher Lifelong Learning Institute (OLLI). And I've given tours of many historical locations here in Fayetteville, including the Square, Evergreen Cemetery, and Wilson (City) Park.

When my time with the different organizations ran their natural course, I went back to my natural course—reading, researching, and

Flashback

Journal of the Washington County Historical Society

Volume 74, No. 3
Fall 2024

John Rollin Ridge
First Native American Novelist

Joachin Murieta, hero of Ridge's novel,
The Life and Adventures of Joaquin Murieta,
the Celebrated California Bandit

writing. I expect to continue doing so until I am no longer able to or the men in white coats capture me in their giant butterfly nets and take me away to where I can no longer do anyone any harm!

Being Bass Boy

ANOTHER OF MY interests after coming home was continuing to be involved in music, playing mostly the upright bass. I had begun playing sometime in 2002 with the encouragement and help of brother Bill. Together with our friends Bill and Jeanette Hill, we formed the band Willow Creek. We mostly played small festivals and the yearly Tinant family get together in western Nebraska along the Niobrara River.

Those were wonderful days, and we made many friends and also had great times playing at the Blood Run Bluegrass Festival in Granite, Iowa, at the Iowa-Minnesota border. Often we were joined there by Lizzie and Mary Tinant, whose family held the Niobrara get-togethers and who I call without irony the Fabulous Singing Tinant Sisters.

Here at home, beginning in the summer of 2008, I had the opportunity to play in our family band East of Zion. My cousin Mac Fultz and his wife Pat put the band together and added their nephew and another of my cousins, Nathan Miller.

In a stroke of good fortune for me, they let me play upright bass in the band. Mac is a terrific lead guitar player. Pat is an amazing singer. And Nathan is a rocket ship mandolin player with tons of energy and creativity. All three of them are talented to the extreme. I like to say I'm the Ringo Starr in this band, super lucky to be there with all those

East of Zion family band, playing at Cane Hill, AR, 2017, left to right: Nathan Miller, Pat Fultz, Mac Fultz, J. B. Hogan (on upright bass).
Photo by Liz Guinn-Miller

skilled musicians and singers. I try to be steady and dependable. Hey, at least it's something!

We started playing at a Firehouse Sub shop on the east side of Fayetteville and progressed from there. Over the next ten plus years we played a lot of fun venues including Hazel Valley Ranch (one show got super rowdy when our crowd decided to start buying us never-ending shots of tequila and such!), Jammin' Java on the Fayetteville Square (for ten straight years), and maybe our favorite of all, the fall Cane Hill Harvest Festival where we played many times including six years in a row from 2014-2019. Like it did for so many other endeavors, COVID-19 brought this streak to an end in 2020 and 2021.

So, for those ten plus years, we steadily put out our positive and mostly upbeat take on Americana music, covering songs by such diverse performers as Kasey Chambers, Patsy Cline, Hayseed Dixie, and the Squirrel Nut Zippers. We played plenty of traditional songs as well. We almost always felt appreciated by our audiences and the feeling was mutual. Looking back, I have to say that my time with East of Zion has been big time fun and a great experience all the way.

First Couple of Books

I WARNED YOU earlier that I would come back to my writing, so don't say you weren't given notice! About 2011, my steady accumulation of stories and poems led to my first deal. Pen-L publishing, a local start-up company run by Duke and Kimberly Pennell, took a chance on me and published my first two books.

2012 saw the publication of *The Apostate*—a novella of the same name and two long stories, all set in the modern desert southwest. The following year, my local baseball history book, *Angels in the Ozarks,* came out. *Angels,* which is still one of my best-selling book to date, tells the story of a professional Class D minor league that existed in Northwest Arkansas and Southwest Missouri back in the 1930s.

Overall, I'm not exactly Mr. Best Seller (trust me on that one) but it beats the heck out of having no publications at all, which is what I had for nearly twenty-five years of writing before I found the electronic literary journals and small presses willing to publish my work. You have to go with what's available to you and that is what I've done.

AS A RESULT of my involvement in local history and the publication of quite a bit of my poetry and fiction, over the last fifteen years I have

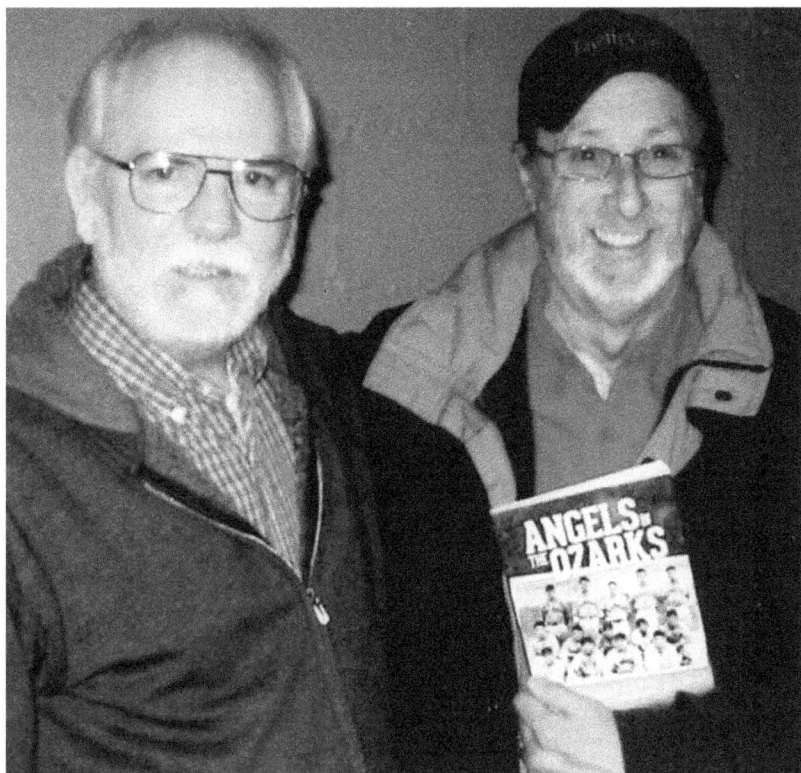

J. B. Hogan with Fayetteville, AR, Mayor Lioneld Jordan, ca. 2014.
J.B. Hogan Collection

given a lot of presentations, tours, and classes. Among these are the history of the Fayetteville Square, Wilson Park—our main city park, old movie theatres, and so on. I have even written and presented on the topic of the 1918 Influenza pandemic (several times and I know, a real pleasant topic). I've also taught courses in fiction, poetry, and nonfiction writing.

Given my innate and slight residual discomfort as either being a part of or in facing crowds, I'm surprised I manage to pull these off. But I have and it's been a real joy to me. For much the better part they have been well received and most of them have been thanks to the OLLI program, the Fayetteville Public Library (with a special thanks to the Reference Librarians, in particular Mickey Clement, Amy Nelson-Lamont, Nancy Brandon, Sierra Nadine Stough, and Cora Hardy-Boland), and my connection to the Washington County Historical Society.

During the COVID-19 pandemic beginning in earnest in early 2020, I wanted to do something productive while we were mostly confined to our homes, so I created some thirty-five or so mini-documentaries on local history. The main series, which I called "Did You Ever Wonder…" consists of thirty-plus videos. A few more videos were done outside the parameters of the series as well.

I'm not a professional videographer, not even close to one, but hopefully the history in the programs compensates for the poor production values. All of the videos are available on YouTube, free for public viewing at any time. Just search on J. B. Hogan and you can see them. Many thanks to the small but appreciative audience for these little shows.

New Publisher

ABOUT THE TIME things were slowing up with Pen-L, a new publisher came calling. Casey Cowan, at the time located here in Fayetteville, was starting up a new publishing company and he sought me out. After several meetings with Casey at Brandon Karn's Jammin' Java and Tiny Tim's Pizza on the Fayetteville Square, I signed a multi-book contract with Oghma Creative Media (now Roan & Weatherford Publishing Associates, based out of Bentonville). With Casey creating top-notch covers and streamlining the editing and publishing process, a string of books ensued.

Living Behind Time, a coming-of-middle-age road trip novel spanning the country from San Diego to Myrtle Beach, came out in late 2014. Two books were published in 2015: *Losing Cotton,* a coming-of-age novel set in California's Imperial Valley, and *The Rubicon,* a collection of many of my poems spiced up with theme-related short stories, mostly of the flash fiction variety.

In the midst of my own books getting published, I helped on yet another book, one that has sold a lot more than any of my individual ones. For several years, I had been bugging my friend and outstanding local historian Tony Wappel to do a book about the Fayetteville Square. This would follow his important books *Once Upon Dickson* with Ethel Simpson and *On the Avenue* with Dennis L. Garrison.

Tony agreed only if I would help on the book and thus from late 2015 through the first half of 2017, we researched and wrote *The Square Book.* It was released that summer and has proven to be popular. I was the "with" on this book and at last count it had done well, moving over 800 copies.

As for myself, two more books came out in 2016. *Fallen,* a collection of short fiction covering a wide range of locales, characters, and stories; and *Tin Hollow,* a novel about a town much like the one the author grew up in but set back when it had its share of racial, economic, and corruption problems during the Great Depression of the 1930s.

One book came out in each of the next two years. *Mexican Skies* in 2017 featured two basically adventure novellas set in, you got it, Old Mexico. In 2018, *Time-and Time Again* was released. It's a time travel book featuring a lumpy, nerdy graphics designer who gets tossed into all sorts of uncomfortable situations in all sorts of times and places.

2020 saw another collection of short fiction published, *Bar Harbor,* but due to the pandemic it was initially available only in online versions. *Bounty Riders,* a western novella, was published in 2021 under the same cover with *Bounty Man and Doe,* also a western novella, by the late, and still popular author Dusty Richards, with whom I had become friends in the latter years of his life.

In the fall of 2023, my local history book *Forgotten Fayetteville and Washington County* was released by Otteford, Roan & Weatherford imprint for nonfiction. The book was very well received and has become my best-selling book so far, of any kind.

Roan & Weatherford has a bunch of my books, new and re-releases, in the print queue. If they publish two a year (new and revised), it will take six years to get all my work out there! Now that's amazing.

J. B. Hogan signing 3-book deal with Oghma Creative Media (now Roan & Weatherford Publishing Associates], Fayetteville, AR, 2015.
J. B. Hogan Collection

The only downside is that I may be so old when the last sets of books come out that I might not even be here to enjoy them or perhaps too enfeebled to appreciate their publication properly! But I'm not going to worry about that, I'm going to stay optimistic and forward-looking.

And speaking of forward-looking, in the year 2028 my hometown of Fayetteville will be celebrating its bicentennial. The two hundredth year anniversary of its founding. That should be a huge celebration. The centennial in 1928 was quite the event and I would hope the bicentennial would be an even grander experience. If I make it till then, that is. I will be going on 83 years old—wow!

Still, I'm hoping I will be around and as a long-time local historian, hope to participate in the festivities in some meaningful way. I always tell everyone that I want to be like E. B. Harrison was back in 1928. Harrison, brother of M. Larue Harrison who commanded the victorious Union forces in the 1863 Battle of Fayetteville, gave the keynote speech when a plaque commemorating the battle in which he was also a participant was dedicated. Mr. Harrison was 88 when he gave his speech, so I could certainly give my own address at 83— even if I have to hobble up to the podium like a worn-out octogenarian might... wait a minute, that's who I would be!

Wrapping it up...
for Now

ALL RIGHT, FRIENDS and neighbors, nowadays I'm a Social Security pensioner and need that government money to live like any other old-timer who didn't make the big bucks in his lifetime. But instead of thinking about retirement and coasting on out of here, I am busier than I have ever been. Most days I put in several hours of work on my own projects, whether writing short stories and poems, researching local history, or cranking out non-fiction works like this one. If I was making any kind of money at all I would probably work even more, but I'm doing enough to keep myself out of trouble—let's hope, anyway.

My late big brother Bill used to remind me that it isn't the completion of the trip, reaching the top of the hill so to speak, that matters so much but the journey getting there. A lot of the time these days I agree with him. When you become an old coot you need to focus on each day that you are given as if it were your last, which it might be.

In the final analysis, it's not so important what people might think about you when you're gone, although that is important to a degree, but what you did while you were here. It's the work that becomes the legacy you leave behind. That's how I see it anyway. It's my current perspective as I head into the early (hopefully) part of what I like to call the end game of life.

My approach is to be sure that I do something daily that moves me forward along my personal, individual journey. It doesn't have to be any great shakes, but each day needs to count somehow. And never stop working, never stop trying. Keep moving, keep going forward. Right up to that absolute last moment when you simply can't do it anymore, right up to the end.

And, so, friends and family, when all is said and done, my final message to you is to say that I appreciate you very much and that I wish you well. Goodbye for now and best of luck on the individual adventure that is your life. Here's hoping I see you around again sometime soon. In the meantime, take care and keep on keeping on. Later, pals.

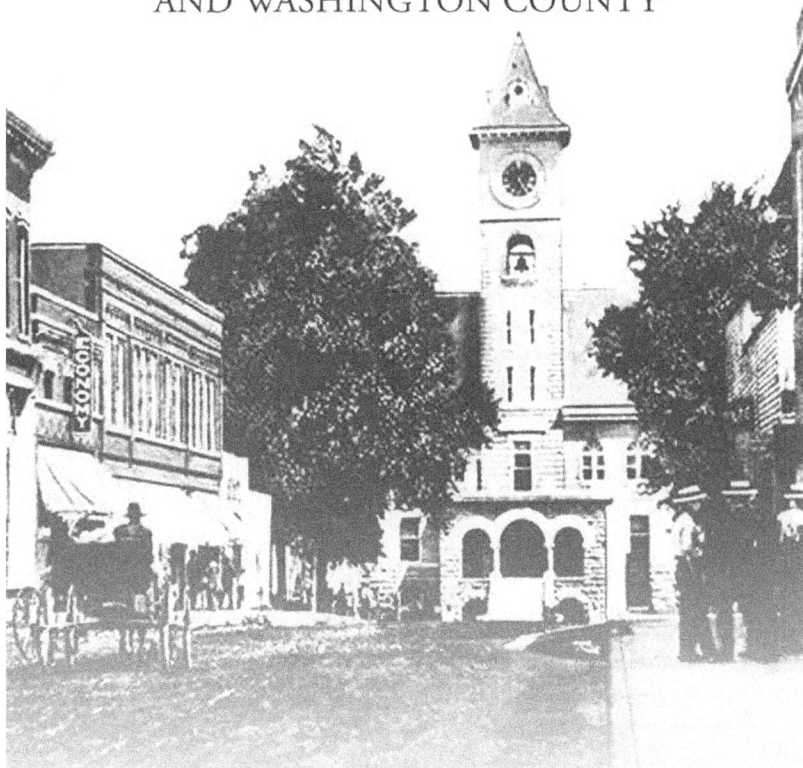

Cover of Forgotten Fayetteville and Washington County, *2023, published by Otterford, an imprint of Roan & Weatherford Publishing Associates. Cover Design by Casey W. Cowan*

J.B. HOGAN is an award-winning author with some 350 stories and poems and twelve books published. Among his books are *Bar Harbor, Mexican Skies, Living Behind Time,* and *Losing Cotton,* He has a Ph.D. in English Literature, worked for many years as a technical writer, and has researched and written extensively on local history. His book *Angels in the Ozarks* is a history of 1930s professional baseball in the area. He helped write *The Square Book: An Illustrated History of the Fayetteville Square* with noted local historian Anthony J. Wappel. His newest local history book, *Forgotten Fayetteville,* was published in September 2023.

www.ingramcontent.com/pod-product-compliance
Lightning Source LLC
Chambersburg PA
CBHW030819090426
42737CB00009B/798